WHEN SHE RISES

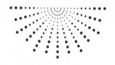

TIFFANY SKIRROW

authors
AND CO.

Disclaimer: Elements of this book is memoir. It reflects each individual
author's present recollections of experiences over time. Some names and
characteristics may have been changed, some events may have been
compressed, and some dialogue has been recreated.

ISBN: 9781099499098
ISBN 13

CONTENTS

DEDICATION

You are the reason I found strength to rise and the reason I continue to.

My hope is that you take this book as encouragement for you both, in the times life tests you or you simply do not understand.

Please know that whatever life throws at you, you have the spirit to emerge from it stronger than ever.

This is my gift to you which is worth more than any material – strength.

To my darling children, Tyler and Sophia-Belle.

FOREWORD

BEFORE SHE RISES

I haven't always felt free.

For years I felt pressed down, suffocated and worthless. I didn't choose the circumstances that made me feel that way, so I didn't consider that I had a choice to feel otherwise. I couldn't see that I had a choice in anything at all.

Anyone who has endured painful adversity or suffering will identify with that feeling of helplessness. When you're out of options and seemingly powerless over your own destiny, there doesn't seem to be a way out. And if low self-worth has been enforced over and over, you feel as if you are the last person with the power to turn things around. I know this place and I know how difficult it can be to envisage a brighter future when it doesn't seem available to you.

I have put together this volume of remarkable stories because I want women to hear a different narrative.

In my darkest moment, I realised I had a choice. I didn't want to live in sadness for the rest of my life. My story was not going to be one of hurt, pain and suffering. In that moment, I chose to believe that life had more to offer me. It was that one decision that changed the course of my life. As I rejected the words that had been spoken over me and the words I had believed about myself, I was choosing instead to write my own.

It is the stories we tell ourselves that define us.

Whatever you are facing, you do have a choice. You do have the power to turn your life around.

As impossible as it might feel when you are in complete despair, I want this book to shine a light on the future accessible to you. You do not have to stay in darkness forever. And you do not have to remain in the grip of that past. All too often I see women living in the shadow of low expectations after their experiences affirm such negative self-perception. It's not an easy road to reignite passion and power when life has left you weary. But I promise you it's not out of your reach.

When one person can turn their own suffering around and even use it as catalyst for success, it becomes a truth for all of us. Whatever truths you have either actively or passively accepted about a future of scarcity or sadness, these inspiring women will show you a new truth.

Each of the women who have contributed to this book have come on their own momentous journey. I approached them because they have come through healing and now stand in the light of their own strength.

and now stand in the light of their own strength.

From this place they can share their whole story as a powerful and inspirational gift to other women who aren't yet on the other side of healing. It takes bravery to lay bare past vulnerabilities and hurt, so I am honoured that these women have agreed to share themselves so completely. From the bottom of my heart I thank and admire the contributors of When She Rises.

My heartfelt desire is that you recognise yourself in the moments of darkness so that you might also recognise yourself in the light. You too can transcend your pain. Your journey doesn't end at the lowest point, there is hope for you to rise also. Hear these women's voices getting alongside you as they say, "I know this pain too". Hold tightly to their words as the women rise, allowing them to lift you also into hope for your next chapter.

This book has a message of power and of grace. We only step into power when we first give ourselves the grace to forgive and rise from our past.

I want to thank my wonderful family for their support throughout this journey. To the women in my family who embody strength and hope, and to honour the part of you which continues to rise. I want to thank my partner David for being so encouraging and brilliantly patient with me throughout this process. I also want to thank my incredible community at 'When She Rises', full of inspiring and incredible women who have made this all possible by believing in me, trusting me and aligning with me on this beautiful journey.

Thank you to the incredibly brave, inspirational, strong and beautiful authors who have found the strength and bravery to step forward in order to be a beacon of light to others through sharing your story. Gifting your message of strength will change lives, thank you for putting faith in me and our mission by gifting us your words.

Lastly, to my children and yours – you are the future, and this is your opportunity to rise.

ABOUT THE AUTHOR

TIFFANY SKIRROW

When she became a mum at 17, Tiffany Skirrow was told that she would never amount to anything. After turbulent teenage years witnessing substance abuse, suffering domestic abuse and the tragic loss of her brother, Tiffany experienced depression, anxiety and eating disorders. Her trajectory looked like another statistical disaster.

Refusing the narrative that society prescribed, Tiffany turned her adversity to triumph. When her son was unexpectedly admitted to hospital with what was believed at the time to be a life threatening illness, and as the bailiffs came knocking, she decisively turned life around.

Now a best-selling author of 'You Are Meant For More'

and the owner of a six figure business, Tiffany offers empowerment and business coaching services to other aspiring female entrepreneurs, equipping them to run their own business and heal through worthlessness, fear and anxiety.

Working with over 400 women globally, Tiffany has dedicated her time to empowering women across the globe to rise up within not just their business, but in life.

And now it's your turn....

ABBY ROWE

*S*ounds super dramatic but I never thought I would be here to see my life unfold the way it has. I always thought that I would follow in my Mum's footsteps. When my Mum was thirty six years old and I was just three, she walked into a road and died shortly after. In my heart of hearts I have always believed that her emotions became too much for her and she decided that this was her only way out. Here is my account of the unfolding of my mental health and how I have learnt to channel the negatives into positives with A LOT of hiccups along the way.

I remember feeling something bubbling in my tummy one day soon after the emptiness appeared. It felt like a ball of something was stuck under my rib cage, swirling and angry. It didn't matter what I did or said it wouldn't go away. The ball would always feel more agitated when my counsellor would ask me questions about how I felt, or what I remembered about Mum. It would squirm and twist until I felt sick and cried. That was my first memory of anxiety. It manifested itself into my life very quickly after losing Mum.

I began to have very vivid nightmares which haunted me most nights. I would see things in my room from my dreams which obviously made me panic. The Dr called them night terrors and said they couldn't hurt me, but this didn't help at night. I was still so young and always terrified to go to sleep as I knew I would wake up not long after and see things. It also affected my eating, to the point that I would be the first at table and the last to leave.

Every time I tried to swallow the food it was like the ball of anxiety stopped it and it came back up. This went on for some time and became a nasty problem. I would have panic attacks before sitting up at the table because I knew what was in store. My family became worried that I would have to be fed through a tube if I didn't start eating. It got a lot worse before it got better but eventually I began to eat small amounts.

After noticing the ball of anxiety had stuck around for a while and caused untold amounts of chaos, the torrents of thoughts appeared. They triggered emotions that I had never felt before. I felt so lost and confused and just wanted my Mum to come back. But of course she didn't. I watched everyone around me go through a plethora of emotions. Mum's death had a ripple effect on everyone and from then on I felt like I was wearing a metaphorical t-shirt that said

"I don't have a mummy". People treated me differently and this stuck with me.

Throughout my childhood I ran into brick walls the size of skyscrapers. A step mum on the scene, brothers being brothers, Dad always working, Nan & Granddad appearing to help as if by magic and still no Mum. I don't remember the exact moment in time that it twigged she wasn't coming home but I do remember that the emotions that were stirring in my head were getting bigger and stronger. I didn't talk much so I didn't explain to anyone what was happening. I felt like I was breaking into a million tiny pieces. I missed her so much.

Without boring you too much about my childhood there are parts that are significant to my story. Like the fact that I was a very creative youngster. I would make things, I would write stories about magic and mayhem and I loved my own company. I spent most of my days in my head, reading, writing in my journal or playing up the hills with my best friend who seemed to understand what I needed without saying a word. We would pretend we were witches and do little rituals that would make my heart feel whole again. Nature made me connect with my Mum's memories somehow. Magic was a HUGE part of my life from then on.

Then there was the bullying, like I said before I felt like I was wearing a t-shirt that said I didn't have a Mum. I swore some kids could see this and they zoomed in on the fact that I was different. I would get called names and I was told I was a bitch just like my Mum was. I felt angry and confused. How did they know what she was like as I didn't even know myself?

These events made me go inwards. I wouldn't talk to anyone about what was happening because somehow I would blame myself for being different. I convinced myself that this was happening because of me somehow. My only real escape from the barrage of emotions was my journal and my books, this little piece of magic would change my life forever.

Whenever the thoughts became too much I would write them down in my journal. I taught myself to be deadly honest, that way they couldn't hurt me anymore. I would always hide my journal from others because it was like an extension of me and I already knew how vile children could be in regards to other peoples misfortunes. I would pour my heart out into those pages most days because it made me feel lighter and more in control of the feelings that were bubbling under the surface.

Sometimes those feelings would burst out uninvited. I would get in trouble if other children were mean to me because I would lash out or start uncontrollably crying. From what I remember it wasn't that much fun being a kid who held onto these emotions that didn't feel like her own.

The older I got the bigger the emotions became. I struggled to communicate the way I felt most of the time, and if I wasn't hiding from big groups of kids I was crying some-where. It was like I couldn't process all these other human beings around me. I could stand in a playground and feel their emotions flying around everywhere, I know this sounds wacky as hell but I knew when someone was sad and they hadn't told me. I could sense things were wrong. Any chance I got I would be looking for animals that needed my help, or I would be sitting under a tree and day dreaming.

I had a best friend throughout school that helped keep me grounded but we played at each other's homes after school more than in school. I found whenever things became difficult my emotions would be heightened and I would find everything hard to manage. Tests, speaking in front of the class, mathematics would send me over the edge if I was asked a question out loud, I was so erratic, but there was no help. I was looked at as a thorn in the side.

This mirrored throughout my high school years. The only thing that changed was the bullying became more intense. I would say I was bullied every single day by the same people. They thought it was funny to make fun of my appearance. Little did they know that their jibes were eating away at me, peeling away any confidence I had with my appearance and making me feel less than worthy. The ball of anxiety would get so big that I would make up excuses not to go into school. I would cry on the way and make up stories of why I was so late, why I couldn't stay and why I didn't do my homework.

I was constantly in trouble; I couldn't concentrate on my school work because I was always being taunted. I stopped writing, I stopped being creative, I stopped eating and I shut down. I would sleep all the through till the next day when I came home from school, because I felt so exhausted all the time. I honestly don't know how I made it through school but I managed to sit some of my exams and then went onto college which I loved with a passion. I was centre of attention for once and for the right reasons. It was a breeze compared to school and I was beginning to find my feet and have a social life at last. I do however remember anxiety still being there, I missed out on trips because I didn't want to travel. I found it hard to sit my exams because I would panic and walk out. Something just didn't feel right.

It got a whole lot worse when I started working. This is when my emotions completely took over. No matter how hard I tried I couldn't keep down a job. I began to self medicate with alcohol which made the anxiety ten times worse. From the age of 16 I have struggled to survive within the working world. I would go to the interview, impress them with my enthusiasm and energy and then give it a few months, I wasn't turning up for work, I was making excuses why I was late, it was like I was a totally different person from when I first started.

I would have panic attacks before starting a shift and some of my managers even thought I was taking drugs (which I never did). This happened in every single job role I had. I felt when I got to a certain point within that job that I needed more. In every job I tried to get into things that kept me challenged and motivated only to be knocked down.

Some of my managers had the belief that I was there to do one job only, they didn't want my ideas.

I was erratic most of the time towards the end. I craved to be challenged and it showed that I was bored. The more people noticed my mood swings the more I became anxious until I became a danger to myself and had to go see the doctor. After nearly a year of therapy, tests and thousands of questionnaires, I was diagnosed with bipolar.

A huge traumatic event, along with other life altering inci- dences, emotions that didn't feel like mine and a distinct pattern that was unravelling within my working life had set my life up to be chaotic, lonely and like the stress button was constantly on. Looking back now I should have realised that the feelings that I felt were being propelled by something that I couldn't control. I must admit when I was diagnosed with bipolar the first time I turned my back on it, I felt so ashamed that they had labelled me. Another t-shirt to wear that said, "CRAZY BITCH!" They handed me over lithium and sent me on my way. I didn't take any meds; I was a complete control freak that steered clear of any kind of drugs. I went about my life like any other 20 something young women would.

Throughout this period I also found out I had one kidney, handy I didn't take the lithium! I lost my granddad to cancer on my mother's anniversary. I ploughed through even more jobs. I stumbled through my life not really thinking I was any different to anyone else. Listening to everyone say "it's normal to feel like that". What was normal about one minute feeling on top of the world like nothing could touch you, and then with the next breath feeling that the only way to stop the thoughts would be to end it! I felt unloved, unworthy and completely chaotic. Up and down like a yo yo, forever scared of my thoughts, anxiety and panic attacks. Spiralling out of control every time I felt the smallest amount of stress.

The breakthrough for me came when I started working for a large corporate company. I really began to notice my episodes the longer I worked there, as this was my longest ever job role. It was like I couldn't hide behind a "normal" mask anymore, the cracks were beginning to show. I remember one day coming into work and not being able to shut down my emotions like I had been told to do by the managers, it was horrendous. People that had seen me always bubbly and happy were seeing the other me. I felt completely overwhelmed and I hyperventilated. No one knew I had been diagnosed with Bipolar, I was ashamed. I would hear people saying, "no one can be that happy all the time".

When I feel pregnant with our boy I seemed to completely calm down. Even though we were being told that we could lose him at anytime because my kidney function was slowly decreasing I felt in control. I was carrying him. I could keep him safe within my tummy because my body knew what it was doing and I didn't even need to think about it. I would take slow walks to work because I knew I didn't have to rush. If I didn't feel great one day I could do some other duties, there was nothing for me to fear at work when I was pregnant. I was happy in life, and at work for once.

After a rushed birth and 4 days in the hospital monitoring my kidney function I brought my bundle of joy home. I thought I would be overrun with love from finally holding my little baby in my arms. I had wished for this day for years. Instead I looked at my baby with complete terror, how was I going to look after my son if I couldn't look after myself. This was when I knew growing up without a mum had affected me severely. I had the over whelming urge to give him everything I didn't get to have.

I wanted to love him more than the world, I wanted to have creative days with him, painting and getting messy, I wanted to be that mum that fed him only organic, but it wasn't meant to be. I struggled. I would look into his eyes and every single piece of me loved him almost too much. I wouldn't leave him alone, I worried about him choking on his food, I worried about him becoming ill, I worried that he was going to be taken away from me. I spent his first year trying to protect him from every single scenario my mind could muster till I had to go back to work.

I would panic when I left him at nursery in case it burnt down. I would rush back from working part time so ready for my cuddles but when I got home with him I felt suffo-cated within the house. It was when I went back to work full time my illness became completely unmanageable. I was working early afternoon till the late evening. I was missing putting him to bed, I wasn't thinking straight when

I was at work. I was having panic attacks and having to explain myself;

It was after my boy was born I began to realise the extent of my illness and what I had been hiding for all those years. My emotions had turned up a notch or ten and I was constantly on edge, all day every day. I managed a few more years at work struggling through the days as I was having sleepless nights. It wasn't until my boy was 4 years old that I asked for help again because my anxiety was taking over.

Another trip to the doctors 10 years later, another six months of therapy and I had another bipolar diagnosis, this time it was rapid cycling. I couldn't do my job properly anymore, I panicked every day. I had to speak to customers, my moods were severely touch and go and I tried everything to stay afloat. To cut a VERY long (and painful) story short I had to leave that company with closed lips and a completely broken heart. I spent the next two years trying to make sense of what had happened over the past six years. I had also lost my Nan during this time, she had been my rock since my Mum had died. I felt the most alone I had ever felt. This was my rock bottom and some of the toughest few years of my life. I had to start again.

All the way through this ordeal I began to realise that I was meant for more. Like I had always believed, but this time it felt stronger and more certain. I had spent so long trying to be heard and now I had the opportunity to start again. But my god it wasn't easy. There was so much inner work to be done that it felt completely overwhelming. This is when I delved back into journaling and writing. My pen became my sword and my words became my magic. Every day I would write down those destructive feelings and emotions and every day I would battle it head on.

It would be the most wonderful story if that was it. I learnt how to live with my illness and I made my dreams come true but that isn't my story. I thought when I left full time employment that my life would get easier but it didn't it got so much worse. I was now totally alone with my thoughts that had haunted me my whole life. I had been going through jobs like they were my plaster, covering up a whirl-wind of untouched emotions that needed channelling into something that would take my mind off feeling so broken.

But every time work became stressful or I lost interest, those emotions would surface. I had always been a thorn in peoples sides my whole life and I didn't want to have to explain myself to people that didn't really give a shit about understanding me. It made me angry at the working world, because no one wanted to understand me. They just saw it as an excuse. If you weren't walking around with your head falling off then you were fine to work, but what they didn't realise was that I desperately needed help.

Being around people on a daily basis was sometimes a blessing but most of the time it was a curse. For me, bipolar manifests into some days I need to be sociable, I needed to vent my soul to my work friends, I needed a reliable shoulder to cry on, I needed routine and I needed to have something to take my mind off the drama that was unfolding in my head. But then other days I would need to be alone, not talk to anyone, not be near anyone and not to take on other people's demons. I couldn't understand myself, why I felt so different one day to the next.

It took a few months to realise that I had fallen into a depressive episode. I made excuses not to go out. I would sit in my lounge with a list as long as my arm of chores but there was no motivation to do anything, not even write. I couldn't understand I had all this time but I felt like I was just wasting it. It took every fibre of my being not to go back to sleep, I vowed I wouldn't fall into this trap as I would be useless to everyone. The more I tried to force doing things the more my brain rebelled. At that point in my life, I didn't feel like I was any use to anyone. I could barely get through the day without the thoughts flooding my brain, having panic attacks and my anxiety going through the roof.

The only consistency in my life was writing and pain. I began journaling again and this time I was deadly honest with myself. I would write every day and started learning to release those deep rooted emotions. I would plan how I was going to make money so I could stay being a flexible happy mummy and help those that needed support and guidance through their own journeys. I made groups on Facebook and taught women to journal which really brought out my confidence. I began making friends with some absolutely awesome ladies that would appear in my inbox and relate to my latest posts.

These people kept me afloat and I will be forever grateful

for their kind words. I was beginning to build a special following of people that listened, appreciated and thanked me. It made my heart sing when I could give someone words of wisdom because I had been through something similar. The more I shared my honesty the more people would interact with me. I would never lie about my feelings again. If I was having an off day then I would write about it, if I had found away to cope with fleeting thoughts and emotions then I shared it. It was a way to connect to people that mattered, and that would read my posts and appreciate my honesty. I don't spend my whole life on Facebook; I have learnt to step away from it now and then because it can become an instant gratification spiral.

While I shared my soul with strangers I began to build my confidence within my writing. I wrote courses that helped women feel less stuck in their life and business. I wrote articles for websites and magazines. I started writing my own books again and getting excited when people asked to read them and gave me feedback that truly blew my mind.

Although I was still in a state of fear and loss of my old life I was starting to create a new life. I was beginning to understand who I was, what I actually wanted from life, and also how to cope with the shit days that would inevitably come back. I didn't hide the fact that I had bipolar. I didn't listen to those that said the way I was thinking and feeling was completely normal. When things got bad, I asked for help. I communicated more with my husband who was seeing a different side to me. I spoke to my family about it and educated anyone that wanted to be in my life on how it felt to live with bipolar and not be on meds.

I look at my life now to what it was all those years ago and I feel blessed, privileged and 100% better equipped to cope with the shit storms that inevitably come with having a mental health issue. I don't let this fact define me, in fact if anything I have learnt to channel my insecurities, bad days and demons into something super positive. After everything I have been through I finally realised that my purpose has risen from this. I knew that I was destined to help others and be someone that made a huge impact in people's lives and that's exactly what I am doing.

With my confidence brimming, my attitude stabilising and my creativity in flow, I decided to really get out of my comfort zone with my books. I had written on and off for years, it was my therapy but now I wanted to share these slices of my life with others. I was always terrified to let someone else read my stories because they reflected the dark times I have had. I have always been attracted to writing about magic, the super natural and anything different and edgy. It is where my heart lies within the writing world. I also came to terms with the fact that I CAN write non-fiction and fiction because the more I shared my work the more people were telling me that there was no mistake, I could write. The belief in my work began to slowly return and I was able to let some of my friends read my stories and also my non-fiction books too. The feedback was amazing. People were asking for more. I was finally making an impact and I loved it.

I would say that writing is my super power, I was gifted this for a reason and it enables me to channel manic and depressive episodes into something that people can read, relate to and enjoy. Ever since I was younger I have always wanted to stir others emotions the way mine would be stirred when I watched or read something that I enjoyed. I wanted to be that person that people looked to for inspiration not only because of my past but because I wasn't afraid to own the past, my flaws and my illness. I think this was the point I finally took off my metaphorical t-shirt and replaced it with... "I am me". I wasn't going to apologise anymore. I finally embraced every single piece of me, the good and the bad bits.

So here I am now, writing this wonderful collaboration with other truly inspirational ladies and looking back on my life thinking, that was hell but it was worth it. I have opened up wounds that I thought I had healed but that's ok because I now take the time to lean into my episodes and find out through journaling, why these are coming up. It will usually be when talking about my past, missing Mum or plain old stress. I have learnt to share my experiences and not take any notice of people's opinions that dim my shine and lower my energy. I have a barrier that I use quite a lot with people that stops me from soaking up their emotions and leaking into my own, making them unmanageable.

At the beginning of this year I was asked to appear in another collaborative book which reached number one on Amazon. I was now a published author and it fuelled me to push forward with my own books. My writing will always be my way of dealing with my past and also dealing with what my future holds for me. I am about to release my first fiction novella that has been a long time in the making.

It has seen me through some horrendous episodes and I am so proud of what I have created. I am now working on the second book and this keeps me going. Release date to come which is beyond exciting. I also have written a self help book on journaling. It is targeted at women that have similar stories to mine. They struggle with their mental health, own or want to own their own business to have financial freedom.

It has practical steps to journal through at your own pace. I LOVED writing this as I wrote it while testing each step myself – awesome book. And I am now writing a book about living with bipolar rapid cycling disorder, the trials and tribulations of trying to not only survive but excel while battling those emotions. Writing is and will always be myself expression and peaceful place.

I have found that my purpose became clearer when I stepped up and owned my shit. That is when I took everything I had learnt myself and applied it to mentoring women/mums that owned their business and struggled with overwhelm, change and feeling constantly stuck. I created a Facebook group where I could help them anyway I could, to not have to go through what I did and feel the way I had felt for so long.

Owning a business and struggling with your mental health

isn't easy to manage and I wanted to be that guide and support for women who suffered like me. I have just launched my activation call where, to put it bluntly, I light a fire under my client's ass and get them to finally feel comfortable about feeling uncomfortable. I am teaching them that stepping out of your comfort zone is the only way to move forward and making your business work.

I am right where I need to be within my journey, and I know that things will only get better. Yes, I will still have episodes, without medication it isn't easy to predict when they will hit but I am becoming more aware of when a shit storm is about to unleash hell over my head. Helping others has always been a core value of mine and when I get messages saying that they have made the amount of money they wanted, or they have fallen in love with an idea that we have brainstormed together, it fills up my emotional piggy bank. I was always told when I started this side of my business that I shouldn't look at my clients as friends; I soon learnt that this just wasn't possible. I care about my clients results. I go above and beyond for them and no one can make me do anything other than the best for them.

When I decided to invest in this project I decided that not only did I want to share my story but I wanted to help shape yours. I wanted to give back something to whoever was reading this and show you that you are not alone, and there are people that care about you and your wonderful gifts. So I created this last section with my ideal client in mind. As I have been harping on for the past thousand words, journaling has helped me shape my life into what it is today.

Throughout my own coaching journey and becoming a hands on mentor and friend to my clients, I have realised that some people are afraid of journaling. They don't know where to start, how consistent they have to be, how to actually start writing, what to write in and also whether they are doing it correctly. The beauty of journaling is that you can make it work for you by being honest with yourself and doing what feels right. There is no right or wrong way of doing this. You will find that it will release barriers that you have had to fight daily. It will air past failures, fears, experiences that have kept you stuck.

It is going to feel slightly uncomfortable as you will be open and vulnerable but working through all the baggage that you have been trailing around will open up more opportunities than you can imagine. And let's face it feeling uncomfortable means you are moving forward. It is becoming more aware of your past and the negative parts of you. Not being afraid of them gives you a power that you have never grasped before. I myself am not bothered about others reading my words because I have done it for so long and I don't have anything to hide from anyone. If you are writing down things that could potentially cause upset be careful with where you store it. This is also where I will tell you that you don't only have to use a notepad or journal for this, if picking up a pen isn't your flavour then get creative with it. Use your computer, cut out pictures or draw what you are feeling.

The first thing you will need to do is go buy a journal that resonates with you. This is so important. If you buy a bulk standard boring ass journal you are not going to want to write in it. If you buy something that mirrors your personality then you are going to be excited about it. The key to this is don't over think it, just go out and buy a journal that you like. I am always drawn to journals that I love working with, seriously I am drawn to A LOT of journals. You don't want to turn this into a chore before we even begin. Once you have found the perfect journal open it and write a date at the top. I know simple right, but there is magic to this. Dating it will become second nature to you and you can look back into your journal to see any patters or dates that are significant.

I prefer to journal at the end of the day so I have something to write about but it really is up to you when you sit down a write. I will always tell my clients and anyone who wants to learn to journal that you need to find your space. Again, it doesn't need to be over thought but finding somewhere that you can easily access builds a connection with that area. You will be able to write no matter what's going on in your head. Some of you may not need a space and can take your journal anywhere, like I do now, but I started with a space that I felt calm in. I would start by talking about how your day has been, where you have been and what you've done.

Once you have written a few sentences start to think about how you have felt that day. Really sit with those feelings and try to explain how they felt. Do not worry about spelling or grammar just write what comes to mind. Then I want you to delve deep. I want you to open up those flood gates and write down everything that is floating around your head on a daily basis. What is bothering you today? What are your fears? Are you feeling anxious? What are your triggers? What have you been hiding from the world? What keeps coming up again and again? This can be painful so be aware of your emotions. Things may come up that you have pushed down for so long that you drain yourself, but this is normal. Think about it as airing your emotions and being able to understand why current blocks are appearing within your life now.

This is how I get everyone starting to journal. I don't say when they should journal because it is personal to each individual. I know myself so well now that I can create journaling prompts that get me to answer why barriers are appearing or why I feel the way I do. You become your own journaling expert and know exactly the type of journaling that helps you be more honest with yourself. Although this is very simple, it is effective and can clear so many negative, reoccurring patterns within your life.

You already know the answer to all the questions that are rattling around in your head, you just have to learn to ask the right question to yourself to get the right answer. I now use journaling as my mini therapy sessions. I know when I need to sit and journal and most days I will journal out at least 8 pages worth of emotions and ideas. It keeps my head as clear as it can be and I do notice a difference when I don't journal. You can add journaling to your morning routine, you can concentrate on just one prompt to get the answers you seek or you can be fluid journaler like me, where you use it as and when you need it.

So ladies that is a shortened version of my story. I feel blessed to be able to share it with the world and alongside some other unique and inspirational ladies that have learnt to channel their negatives into positives. I am now a person that embraces her flaws isn't afraid of failing because there is a lesson in every single one. I don't apologise for being me because I know I am different, and I love that. I am soul centred, spiritual, woo woo and sometimes completely mad, but I wouldn't have me any other way.

ABOUT THE AUTHOR

ABBY ROWE

"Life is the greatest teacher"

Over the years Abby Rowe has taken on many roles, author, influencer, mentor, mother, wife and all round free spirited mad women.

She tends to push the boundaries when it comes to labels and rarely holds onto one description.

She has been known to share her experiences with her mental health ensuring others know they are not alone.

She journals and writes every chance she gets because she has found that it helps her express herself and her imagination is her secret weapon.

Abby is honest, ambitious and is always working towards her big dream of making her mark on the worlds through her words and has a gift of being able to inspire others to push their own boundaries.

Abby is currently working on a few projects at the moment because she finds that focusing on a handful of ventures helps ease her bipolar episodes. She is in the last stages of finishing the two books she is working on.

One is a self help book that will teach women in business to journal and manage their mental health and the other is a fictional tale of creatures, witches, magic and fallen angels. Holding nothing back, Abby will be releasing both books within 2019. She is also getting ready to launch her brand new journaling course on Udemy, plus she is looking into creating her own journal collection.

Throughout Abby's life she has worked with mums, women in business and women who struggle to manage their mental health. She helps them create a life and business that they love by leading by example. She is never afraid to be open and vulnerable and believes that sharing her story will enable other women to learn to shine their light, find their voice and make their mark on the world.

Changing people's lives is one of Abby's top priorities, whether that's through her Facebook groups, activation calls, one to one mentoring, journaling courses or through her content. She is known for her kind nature and desire to help anyone who needs it, going above and beyond their expectation.

With experiencing a childhood trauma and thinking she

was going to follow in her mother's footsteps most of her life, she has managed to channel her negatives into positives all through the power of writing and consistently believing in herself and her purpose.

Abby has been known to say that she lives a double life due to having bipolar; she can't take medication as she also has kidney disease so she manages through her writing and through her own spiritual practise. Her energy has been known to be contagious and women that have worked with Abby have described the connection to be a creative and high vibe relationship.

Abby is the first to admit that when there is light there is also darkness and this can come in the form of depression and anxiety. It has been a never ending battle from a young age but she manages, adapts and always comes out more knowledgeable and stronger than before.

Abby can be found on her Facebook profile:

https://www.facebook.com/abby.kedwell

Also within her new group:

https://www.facebook.com/groups/2287254711488469/

 facebook.com/abby.kedwell

The power of 3 - Understanding the three brains - my journey through trauma

Section 1 : The elephant in the room

"Trauma is the most avoided, ignored, belittled, denied, misunderstood and untreated cause of human suffering. Trauma is like a shock. It's like a shock to the psyche, it's a shock to the body, it's a shock to the nervous system, it's a shock to the spirit and the soul. It's a shock that just cuts right through us and often cuts us in pieces"

Peter Levine - "Healing Trauma"

I have known for years that my purpose on this planet is to raise awareness around trauma and how it affects our lives, only it's taken years for me to get to the place where I can fully own my story. It's been a rollercoaster ride to get to that place where I no longer feel the need to apologise to anyone for speaking my truth. Where I no longer instinctively shrink back for fear of being judged by others for sharing my journey. To stay in my lane and not speak out about a topic that is still misunderstood by so many and perhaps considered "taboo" by some, would mean I would be doing a disservice to the thousands of people who for many reasons have not yet found or used their voice.

My story is for those very people. Those who do not have the awareness or the understanding of post traumatic stress and have wrestled with debilitating symptoms for years, trying desperately to hide it, fade it or fix it. Those who think they have dealt with traumatic events only to find that they still have triggers and they simply cannot seem to "shake it off" and move forwards with their lives. Those who perhaps are living in third world countries, those far flung places across the globe where they have no access to suitable treatment. It is for those individuals that I choose to share my story.

Trauma has been a part of my life since I was 10 years old when I was faced with the sudden and unexpected death of my mother. This was followed three years later by a motorbike accident, in which my 19 year old sister was killed. Years later when I was in my twenties I was involved in a terrorist attack in a church in Cape Town, followed soon after by a traumatic family murder and thereafter the suicide of my best friend .

Tony Robbins says this "Life is going to come for you whether you like it or not. It's not what happens to you that's important but how you choose to respond"

With every death, every dramatic event, every calamity, every unbearable loss came the aftermath.

The shock, the grief, the confusion, the anxiety, the brain fog, the muddled thinking, the head noise, the unanswered questions, the questioning of my faith in God, the search for meaning, the deep sense of my life spiralling out of control,

again, and again, the blows came and all I could do was cling on for dear life, all the while trying desperately to make some sort of sense of it all.

Trauma became the elephant in the room for me, lurking in the shadows. Whilst I cannot say that trauma has defined my life, I can say, with certainty, that it shaped my journey. It tore through my life like a tornado, it sucked me up, then spat me out. It dug its claws into the very core of my being, teasing me, pushing me, challenging me to seek, to search, to change. For years I had such a shaky sense of self. I felt like I was constantly reacting to events that were outside of my control and that made me feel both powerless and helpless.

It was only when I reached the point where I had worked through and reprocessed the trauma that I was fully able to accept it, embrace it, release it and reframe it.

During my research into PTSD I noticed how varied the

definitions for this condition are. A multitude of different perspectives exist and whilst it's true that there is a "spectrum" of intensity and severity with this condition, I do believe that we have a long way to go in fully understanding this condition.

The NHS defines PTSD this way "An anxiety disorder caused by very stressful, frightening or distressing events";

Wikipedia says it's "a mental disorder that can develop after a person is exposed to a traumatic event";

The free dictionary speaks about a "debilitating, psychological condition triggered by a trauma",

Elise Cooper wrote in the American Thinker in 2017 "PTSD is an emotional and silent wound that is not out there for people to see. The stereotype is still alive and well, where many associate it with being a lunatic".

The definition that most resonates with me, following what I have learned from my own research and personal experience is best described by PTSD UK who say "PTSD is essentially a memory filing error caused by a traumatic event",

I dislike the word "disorder" as it does not accurately describe the condition. It is for this reason that I choose to call it post traumatic stress. Post traumatic stress is NOT a disorder. It is a NORMAL response to an abnormal situation.

For years I did not understand my symptoms, the recurring

leg tremors, the tendency to avoid situations that reminded me of the traumatic events, difficulty in concentrating, sleeping with the light on, feeling fearful in crowded places. I would spend a lot of my time in the "fight, flight, freeze" zone - that place where your entire nervous system automatically goes into high alert when triggered.

It was only when I began to study NLP, the work of Peter Levine (somatic experiencing) and more recently heart math, that I began to learn HOW and WHY trauma gets stored in the body where it can sometimes remain for years. Over time our conscious memories fade and heal, however, the body doesn't forget. Our bodies cannot express themselves in words, so they respond with physical sensations. Tremors, shaking, muscular tension, fatigue, detachment, difficulty in concentrating.

These symptoms kept resurfacing for many years after the traumatic events, often at the most inopportune times. For years I believed that there was something seriously "wrong" with me. I felt ashamed for being unable to control how I was feeling. This self-loathing and sense of shame is something that I have observed in many others who suffer with PTSD.

I struggled with a deep sense of shame. I felt ashamed that I could not control my symptoms. The battle was between my rational mind (that would tell me time and time again to "get over it" and "get on with it") and my emotions - fear, guilt, shame, helplessness, detachment, exhaustion.

God works in mysterious ways and I truly believe in divine

timing. I sought solace in my faith. My prayers weren't sophisticated or scripted and mostly went something like this "Please help!" this was usually at 2am when I had woken from a nightmare and felt frozen with fear. The answer came years later and in a completely unexpected way. It came the day I had one of those huge life-changing "aha moments" which I now define as being the start of my healing journey.

I distinctly remember that exact day in June a few years back, sitting with a therapist friend of mine in her back garden, telling her about my experiences and how raw they still felt (even though many years had passed since the events). As I relayed to her my story, I instinctively placed my hand over my heart, something I had done many times before over the years.

It was as if a physical ache still existed somewhere deep in my chest. She looked at me and I will never, ever forget what she said "Ali, that's your heart brain. That's where all your emotions gets stored and your memories get processed. It's a different part of your brain to your rational brain". In that very moment it was as if a light had been switched on in my mind. No one had ever told me that I had three brains before!

I rushed home and began to research the "three brain" theory. I read all I could find about the lizard brain and the mammalian brain and how the fight, flight, freeze response works. I felt like I had won the lottery! I had found my answer to "what's wrong with me".

Why on earth had no one told me about this before? I truly believe that day was the turning point for me. I gained huge amounts of self-awareness over the next few weeks during my research, which became the first step for me in allowing myself to FULLY heal. I had found my answer. My heart brain needed to heal. I had figured out WHAT needed to happen. Now I just needed to figure out HOW.

A little while later I wrote a blog post titled "The day I fell in love with my heart brain". Oh what an enormous sense of relief I felt in writing that blog post! Hope had begun to rise in my heart and I knew that I was going to be okay.

Section 2 : Tremors and night terrors

My post traumatic stress journey began on Sunday night 25 July 1993. I will never forget the weather that night - cold and rainy - a typical winters evening in Cape Town. My friend and I were late for the church service at St James church in Kenilworth and I remember that split second decision we took to enter the building through the back door. It was late, and after all it was raining.

We ended up sitting towards the back, at the far left of the building. Midway through the service, two young singers came up to the stage to start a duet. I recall hearing the start of the song then somewhere in what seemed like the distance, I remember hearing a pop-popping sound. I felt bewildered and at first I could not comprehend that shots were being fired. Suddenly someone was yelling for everyone to get down and take cover.

Four masked gunmen yielding R4 assault rifles had burst through the front doors of the church and opened fire on the congregation of some 1000 people. Men, women, teenagers and children were in the line of fire - people were pinned to the floor, frozen in terror, unsure whether they were going to live or die. As I lay there, unable to move, I heard a loud explosion, followed shortly by another. I became aware of a sensation covering my hair. I wondered if it was blood, then realised much later that it had been the falling dust and debris caused from the two M26 hand grenades exploding.

Shock has a protective effect on the psyche. After that initial adrenaline surge - the dry mouth, the pounding in my chest, the feeling of being frozen, my world became foggy and hazy. My brain had taken me into a massive, misty bubble. I felt dazed, I felt disorientated and discon-nected, as if I was watching a movie of events unfolding.

After I got up off the floor I became aware of people sobbing. I felt numb and detached . Somewhere in the distance I could hear the sound of sirens. I still don't recall what I physically saw thereafter and perhaps I saw a lot more than my unconscious mind has allowed to resurface. This is something I explored a lot in my therapy with EMDR. For a while it really bothered me!

Why could I not remember more? I distinctly remember the noises of the guns and yet no screaming. I don't remember myself screaming and perhaps I could not speak. I now realise that remembering the detail is not the important part in healing trauma. What's important is how our brains process the memories that we do have.

Memory suppression is our subconscious minds way of protecting and preserving us. It was only when I saw the media footage of the aftermath a few days later showing the debris strewn church, with remnants of the pews that had been ripped apart and images of blood soaked carpets and corpses, that I began to realise the magnitude of the devastation that had been caused that night.

I became acutely aware of my own mortality and how little control I actually had over my own fate. I recall feeling intensely grateful that I had survived and yet at the same time there was an overwhelming sense of guilt . Guilt that I had survived whilst others had died. Guilt that I had left the building soon after and had not stayed to help others .

11 people died that night and 58 were injured. A group of Russian seamen who had been visiting SA, had been attending the service as part of a Christian outreach program. One of the seamen lost both legs and an arm in the attack. Some lost eyes, limbs and sustained other life changing injuries. Some lost spouses and children that night. For me it was an experience that would truly shape my life forever.

The perpetrators of the attack were members of APLA, the military wing of the Pan African Congress in South Africa. 1993 was a year of political turmoil, tension and unrest in the country, the year before Mandela was released from prison. Five months later APLA carried out a second attack on a pub in Cape Town where four students were killed.

Terrorist attacks can never be justified and the APLA, like most terrorist organisations had focused on soft targets. St James was a multiracial church which was heavily involved in projects in the most deprived townships in Cape Town. Outreach, serving the community and the poor was at the heart of what they stood for.

On that night the congregation was a mix of all nationalities including a large eastern European community. I later learned that the chief of the terror group had given orders for the killers to torch the building that night. Their intent was for everyone to be killed.

There happened to be one man in the congregation that night who had been carrying a hand gun and if it wasn't for him, I may not have been writing this story The incredible bravery of this man who took it upon himself to stand up to 4 men who were wielding automatic rifles was truly remarkable. He began firing back, taking the gunmen by surprise and causing them to flee, leaving behind a broken and devastated community.

In the weeks that followed the attack on St James, there was an outpouring of forgiveness from the Christians who had suffered at the hands of the attackers. There is tremendous power in the act of forgiveness and I truly believe that it is the first step towards healing. To quote the late, great Nelson Mandela "Forgiveness liberates the soul. It removes fear. That is why it is such a powerful weapon".

It was only days later when I began to emerge from my "shock" bubble that my body began to shiver and shake. I seemed to be in a constant state of hyperarousal. I was jumpy, irritable and tearful. I could not relax. I did not want to leave the house or be alone. My descent into the hell that is post traumatic stress had begun.

In the days and months after St James I was in constant survival mode. Fear had moved in to my heart and it was exhausting. Not the "butterflies in your tummy" type of fear but the raging, gut-wrenching fear that seems to take a hold of you at the level of your soul. I remember a few years back taking my son to the emergency room when he was around 5 years old. He had developed acute earache and was visibly distressed.

The nurse showed him a series of faces to help him to describe the pain he was feeling. The faces ranged from 1 - being a very happy smiley face meaning I'm feeling fine, to 10 - which was a very sad, crying face, meaning this hurts a lot. He was able to point to the face which showed how painful his ear was so that they could treat him accordingly.

If you could measure fear on a similar scale I would say that every time I felt afraid during those months, the intensity of that sensation would quickly surge to a 10 irrespective of what the trigger was. Night times were the worst. I would go to sleep, only to wake in the middle of the night in full flight, fight or freeze mode, heart pounding in my chest, thoughts racing, every muscle in my body clenched. I would turn on all the lights, lock my door and sometimes sit there for hours feeling totally consumed by, and sometimes physically sick with fear, eventually falling asleep again in the early hours and waking up feeling totally depleted.

Shame seems to be common with post traumatic stress sufferers. I felt ashamed to admit my feelings to those around me. I felt embarrassed that I was unable to "snap out of it". The medication which my doctor had prescribed produced a highly sedating effect. I could not bear feeling light headed and spaced out most of the time, needless to say I did not continue with the medication.

The cycle continued for months on end. I felt on edge in crowded places . I felt uneasy in shopping malls and the sound of exploding fireworks reminded me of automatic gunfire. Getting back to normality felt like a mammoth task. How did one get back to normal after something like that? My sense of security in the world had been shattered and I did not know how to ground myself again. I went through the motions, I had bills to pay, I had responsibilities like everyone else. I went to therapy for a while and saw no point in simply going through the whole story again and again. I know now that there is no such thing as getting back "to normal" after trauma. Trauma changes us permanently. Instead, we need to find our new normal.

A year later I took a few months out to go travelling before moving to the UK permanently. Life was awash with fresh opportunities - new jobs, new friends and exciting new adventures to be had along the way. I spent three wonderful months seeing the US before heading to London where I moved into a shared house with friends, started dating a new man and got a job as a beauty therapist in a thriving salon . Life was fun! I had a great social life and the novelty of living in a new country was a welcome distraction.

I was at work one day when I received a phone call late one afternoon. My sister was crying on the phone as she explained to me that my step-brother who had been travelling abroad on a business trip at the time had been reported missing. He had not arrived back home, and contact had been made with the police in the country where he had travelled to. After a thorough police investigation, my family were informed that a body had been discovered and this was later identified as being my brother's.

The killer was tracked down, arrested and imprisoned and it was later discovered that this same man had been responsible for multiple murders across the world. I was once again transported back to my familiar old "shock bubble". This little bubble that made me feel detached and numb with disbelief was a place to escape to. Again it was as if this whole scenario was playing out on a movie screen somewhere in the distance. I cannot describe how horrific the next few weeks were for my family. Murders did not happen in normal families; this was the stuff that movies were made of. Surely this could not be happening to us?

One of my mentors once said this to me a while ago and it

really struck a chord. I was attending a presenting work-shop in London and was busy sharing my story with the audience. I began to go into the finer details. I wanted to make an impact after all! As I was speaking, he stopped me mid-flow and I will never, ever forget his words to me. He said "Alison, there is something I would like you to remember. Your self worth does not and will never depend on the amount of pain you have suffered".

Up until that point I had felt the need to highlight the gory bits as a way of justifying my pain. When we tell our trauma stories, what we are effectively saying is "I want you to see me, I want you to notice how much pain I have had", I no longer feel the need to do this. My intention is to empower others by creating awareness. This is what drives me to share my story.

Weeks turned into months and "normal life" resumed after my brother's death. Just like that, my beautiful stoic family kept going. We were so good at that, in fact we had become experts at that over the years. You swept things under the carpet, you picked yourself up and you just kept going. You had to keep going. One day at a time, I would say to myself repeatedly. Just one day at a time...

Section 3 : Dark night of the soul

I had some wonderful friends during this time who rallied around and there was one in particular, who really stood out for me. We had been friends since our late teens and she was the one person who truly "got me" I remember the nights out dressed up to the nines, knocking back shots in student bars, partying hard into the early hours, dancing until our heads hurt and our feet ached.

Then there were the girly nights in with face masks, nail polish and late night movies. Bitching about men and love affairs gone wrong, mending each other's broken hearts and sharing our deepest secrets and dreams. The philosophical debates into the early hours of the morning, putting the wrongs of the world to rights! The spiritual conversations - discussing God and the meaning of life.

Oh, how I remember those days! The music festivals in Hermanus, falling asleep on mattresses under the stars with not a care in the world. I treasure the memories, the good times, the fun, the side-splitting laughter that made my belly ache. She was my soul sister, my greatest confidante - the one who could read what I was thinking without me ever having to say a word. She was the best friend I have ever had.

Her name, in another language, means "little girl" and this is exactly who she was. Strong willed, feisty, intelligent, playful ,determined, business like, driven and super confident. There was also the side she kept hidden - sensitive, vulnerable, fragile. In essence a little girl. The little girl who had been sent to boarding school when she was five years old, the little girl with the free spirit and the wild heart who longed to be held and loved. The little girl who battled demons that nobody knew about.

I've heard depression being referred to as "the dark night of the soul". My friend knew about those dark nights - sometimes she would journey there and those were the times when she would become sad, low and confused. It was during those dark nights when she would question everything - her relationships, her career, her friendships, whether she fitted into the world. It was somehow hard for me to reach her when she was there in that place and intuitively I understood this about her.

She was deep, my beautiful friend. And deep people have many, many layers. Layers that are hard to break through. She often mentioned that she felt depressed and I remember her telling me once that she had visited a therapist who had told her that she was "too brittle" to respond to treatment.

Life is so very fleeting and fragile and yet we all live like it's never going to end. Each moment is precious, it shouldn't be wasted, every second a memory that needs to be captured and held in the heart like treasure. If there was one single weekend that I wish I could re-live it would have been, without a doubt, that one trip when I visited South Africa. That one week in April that I spent with my friend. After I had relocated to the UK, our friendship had taken on a slightly different course.

We had spoken often on the phone during those 2 years since I had been away, even though our lives were poles apart. I shared my travelling adventures, she shared her experiences of newly married life. I went home for visits and we picked up our friendship exactly where we had left off. It was as if no time had passed in between. I remember one particular weekend when we had the best time ever. It never occurred to me that week would be the last time I would ever see her again.

It was 5 months later when I got the phone call from my Dad that would shatter my world all over again.

My gorgeous friend had taken her life. My beautiful, intelligent friend who had everything going for her, had in the prime of her life, put a trigger to her head and ended it in an instant. The next few days were excruciating for me after I discovered messages which had been left on my answerphone only days before. Messages left two nights in a row when I had been out.

I played those message a hundred times over, I tried to detect the tone in her voice. Those messages haunted me for years on end. I went over those messages a hundred times with my therapist, I sobbed over those messages. My emotions fluctuated between anger (at myself and her) agonising grief and excruciating guilt in equal measure. There were the countless "what ifs". What if I had been there to answer those messages? What if I had been able to speak to her? What if I had been at home those evenings that she had rung? What if, what if, what if ....

"Suicide carries in its aftermath a level of confusion and devastation that is beyond description" ∼ Kay Jamison.

Suicide is tough. Period. There will always be unanswered

questions and I'm okay with that now. I know that if I was able to speak to my friend right now, that she of all people, would have wanted me to let go, she would have wanted me to be free.

Grief is not a linear process. It comes in fits and starts. During those next few months I ached with pain - there was a heaviness in my chest that was unbearable and yet I refused to let myself break. I could not go there. I was trapped in fight, flight, freeze mode. I was a survivor. I had to go to work, pay my bills, put on a brave face and "keep my chin up" I had to keep going!

Post traumatic stress is the silent wound and those who suffer become expert at surviving. I developed strategies. Somedays I would detach and go into my "numb bubble". Then there were the days when the tiniest things would trigger me, and I would become hypervigilant.

I remember once going for minor surgery. When I was waiting for the anaesthetist to administer the pre-med, my legs began to tremor uncontrollably, so much so that the consultant noticed and was intrigued by it. I remember feeling proud of my strength and my ability to "persevere" no matter what. Night times were a different story though. Waking up with my heart pounding in my chest, feeling terrified was the norm. For years I slept with the light on. It helped me to feel safe and somehow better able to cope with the night terrors.

Years later my therapist explained to me that it's during our sleep when the subconscious mind processes/tries to process our experiences. Dreams/nightmares are a tell-tale sign that the trauma is playing on a loop. A peaceful nights sleep for me was rare. Needless to say, I felt drained and exhausted much of the time. For years I hid my struggles. I felt ashamed to admit how scared I felt and that I needed help. I was raised in a family where it was normal to hide your emotions. I was raised in a generation where the expectation was for you to "get on with it". "TIME WILL HEAL", is what everyone would tell me.

Section 4 : Opening up the treasure chest

Fast forward many years and I am proof that statement is simply not true.

Time does not heal, awareness heals.

Following the suicide of my beloved friend, I began psychotherapy sessions with a lovely London based thera-pist. At the time I was in a difficult and volatile relationship and there was much to talk through during those sessions. I stayed in therapy for just under a year. Did it help me? Absolutely. Having a safe place to talk about your issues where you are not going to be judged is empowering and enlightening and of course that helps. However it did not completely cure my traumatic stress symptoms.

Awareness heals.

Embracing and understanding the heart-brain and how it responds to stress, heals.

That day in June sitting and chatting in my friends back garden was the start of my healing journey. My new found revelation around the workings of the three brains was the turning point. The awareness I gained was the golden key I had been looking for, which would unlock the secrets of my wonderfully complex and highly efficient brain. Hungry for knowledge, I began to study NLP, qualifying as a practitioner and coach. I haven't looked back since. NLP stands for Neuro Linguistic Programming and is "the study of how we think and communicate with ourselves and others".

On the first day of the training, my tutor asked us to use a metaphor to describe our expectations of the course. I remember describing an image of myself opening a treasure chest which was filled with shimmering jewels, necklaces and an array of precious gemstones, shimmering in the most unusual and beautiful colours. "Studying NLP for me", I said, "is going to be like discovering precious jewels for the first time. I am going to treasure everything I learn, for within that lies the key to unlocking all that has held me back and kept me in pain for so long".

Learning exactly how our brain works and why we respond the way we do, was key for me in order to facilitate my own healing. I learnt so much about the unconscious mind and the mechanism of the stress response. I learned powerful tools - exercises and techniques that I could use to change my neurological state in the moment, to calm anxiety or to master my emotions in the moment.

I learned about the power of language and self-talk and

how to change language patterns in order to produce different outcomes. I learned about anchoring and reframing, timeline therapy and hypnosis. I learned how to trust my gut brain a lot more, how to tap into my intuition and listen to what that still, small voice was saying to me.

During my NLP practitioner training, odd things began to happen to me. The twitching in my legs which had begun after the terrorist attack resurfaced. Each night during my course, I would fall asleep with twitching and a sensation of intense heat in my legs. I developed a tightness in my neck and shoulders. I felt that my unconscious mind was letting me know that it was still holding on to trauma in my body.

It was signalling to me that there was unfinished business and I sensed that I had more work to do . This time therapy was different as I knew so much more about my beautiful brain. And what's more I had fallen in love with this beautiful, resilient old heart - brain of mine. I wanted to nurture it and give back after all the hard work it had done for me, keeping me safe over the years. This time I WANTED therapy. In fact I ran to therapy. This time instead of resisting it, I embraced it.

And so, I began my journey with EMDR (eye movement desensitisation and reprocessing)

EMDR is the NICE approved treatment for PTSD in the UK and involves generating one type of bilateral sensory input such as side to side eye movements or hand tapping in order to allow the traumatic memory to be processed effectively.

I cannot say that it was easy. In fact the first few sessions were akin to running a marathon in the figurative sense. I felt emotionally battered and drained. I was revisiting all those painful memories, only this time with EMDR I was allowing my brain to reprocess them in an appropriate way. After a few sessions, I began to feel lighter, almost as if layers were coming off. As a reptile has to shed its skin before new growth can be visible, I intuitively knew that this was an integral part of my journey to freedom. I journaled a lot during that time. I brain dumped all the emotion, all the thoughts, feelings and experiences that came up for me during my period of therapy. I nurtured my heart, I honoured my emotions and gave myself the space to heal.

This time I co-operated with my heart. I allowed for the ebb and flow, in fact I embraced all of it. All the years of stuffing the anxiety down and "putting on a brave face" had been exhausting. Therapy for me was liberating because I didn't have to pretend anymore. There was no one to judge me, no one to berate me for behaving a certain way. I could finally surrender to the healing process and be free!

I noticed changes .....

Far less teeth grinding, no more leg shaking and twitching, peaceful nights sleep.

News of terror attacks in other parts of the world no longer triggered me.

Daily stressors began to trigger me less.

I began to feel more resilient.

More confident.

Less afraid of being judged.

More determined to set better boundaries for myself.

And more determined to follow the inner guidance of my heart.

And to begin to live and speak my truth.

The day my therapist discharged me I felt a surge of joy,

I had graduated!

I had come full circle and was now equipped and ready to help others move on from trauma.

Knowing what I now know about the brain and have experienced firsthand, I am absolutely convinced of the following:

We cannot fix post traumatic stress by getting on with it".

We cannot fix post traumatic stress by "hiding it or suppressing it.

We cannot fix post traumatic stress by rationalising it.

We cannot fix post traumatic stress by simply talking about it.

We overcome post traumatic stress by accepting where we are and admitting that we need help.

We overcome post traumatic stress by honouring our heart brain.

That deep subconscious part of ourselves that controls 90% of our behaviour.

All human emotions are stored in the heart.

The only way to treat ANY type of emotionally rooted issue such as traumatic stress, anxiety or depression is by undergoing therapy that causes change at the level of the heart. The fastest route to deep unconscious change is only through the heart .

NLP, Hypnotherapy, EMDR, HMS (Heart mind centred therapy) and heart/brain math - all of these therapies work to cause change at this deeper unconscious level - this is where the stress response generates and this where reprocessing occurs.

Martin Webster, ex-soldier, PTSD expert. NLP master practitioner and founder of HMS therapy says the following, "Looking in your own mind for an emotional problem is like looking in the boot of your car when the engine has failed, It simply will not work. Healing the heart is the absolute key".

A little while back I got a tattoo on my right arm that says "courage"

As a small reminder; It takes courage to ask for help

Brene Brown says "Courage doesn't mean you don't get afraid; courage means you don't let fear stop you".

My tattoo is a symbol of my journey, it signifies a rite of passage for me, it signifies that it's time for me to move on to the next phase of my journey, which is to take my message to the world.

There is no shame in going through trauma.

Post traumatic stress is a normal reaction to an abnormal situation.

Post traumatic stress is a condition of the heart.

And the heart has tremendous capacity to heal, as it has to love.

A friend of mine said to me a few years back "Ali you have had such a tragic life, how have you coped with all of this?"

Now my response would be to reframe that statement and I would say :

"I've had a beautiful and colourful life with tragic circumstances".

It's not about what has happened that matters, it's about how we reframe what has happened and the meaning the we give to it.

ABOUT THE AUTHOR

ALI SMITH

Ali's career began in the health and fitness industry where she worked as a fitness instructor and gained qualifications in nutrition and also as a Pilates teacher.

She has also worked in commercial business development and sales roles within the healthcare and pharmaceutical industries, and is a self-confessed research geek!

She is a trauma-resilience coach, NLP practitioner, speaker and presenter, helping people to find their voices, own their stories, and step into their new normal after trauma.

She is super practical, intuitive and outcome focused in her approach, drawing on her own experiences with trauma and post traumatic stress.

Ali is on a mission to raise awareness of post traumatic stress, removing the stigma and shame often associated with the condition.

You can find Ali at www.ali-smith.com

facebook.com/AliSmithtraumaresiliencecoach

instagram.com/alismithcoaching

3

ANGELA PEART

THE POWER OF SELF-RECOVERY

*E*arly years

I was born in the North East of England into a man's world. The youngest sister of three older brothers, I spent my childhood wanting to be part of their gang. They all shared a room, and as the only girl, I had the luxury of my own room, but it always made me feel like the outsider. I always wanted to be like them and although I had to recognise that I could never be, I still spent my childhood trying to keep up, trying to do everything that they did – climbing trees, riding bikes.

My mum was a powerful woman, she worked hard all her life to give us the best life she could, although she didn't suffer fools gladly and I sometimes think that's where I get my strength to keep going from. Being the only girl of the four, it was inevitable that I would be a daddy's girl, born on the twenty-fifth of December, he always said I was the best Christmas present he could have ever had. It is safe to say that my dad is my hero.

Going to senior school emphasised the difference between us again, my brothers had gone to school just down the road with all their friends. My mum however felt that wasn't the best school for a girl, so decided to send me to what had been the Girls High School which had recently become a comprehensive. On the first day of senior school, when all my friends were going down the road together, she took me on the hour-long journey using two buses to the other side of town and left me outside the school gate, all on my own. I knew no-one, and everyone else there had all their junior school friends with them, so weren't interested in me. I didn't fit in because I wasn't from around there and spent my school years struggling to make close friends, although it wasn't all bad because I met my first love Stewart there, more on that later.

I didn't have a great time at school in many ways, and I ended up leaving at sixteen with no qualifications, keen to get into the world of work. My first job was in a supermarket, working on the tills and stacking shelves. I didn't mind the work, itself, but hated my manager. He was truly old school and thought that his word should be law and that this precocious girl should simply do as she was told, enthusiastically and without question. This approach never worked well, and it came to a head early one morning before the shop opened, the floors needed cleaning and he ordered me to mop them, rather than ask those standing around drinking tea. Never short of confidence (and possibly unwisely), I told him where to stick his mop, threw the overall at him and left him open mouthed as I marched out.

At sixteen I didn't know that he had actually done me a favour by showing me how not to manage people as all that was on my mind was how to tell my mother what I had done.

Around the same time, I met the man who was to become my first husband. I'd been with my first love Stewart for about two years when he met another girl and he left me. I was devastated, I had thought we were meant to be. On the rebound and determined to show Stewart the mistake he'd made, I threw myself at a man in his twenties who, with his money and greater life experience swept me off my feet. I got in too deep, too quickly and before I knew it we were married and on the property ladder, planning children.

One of the admin jobs that followed the supermarket was the first time that I found that work could be fun. The company rented pay-as-you-go TVs fitted with a coin slot, each customer's home had to be visited once a week to empty the meter and I loved the interaction with people and the camaraderie that I developed with my colleagues, one of whom was to become my lifelong friend and rock in times of crisis.

I got to meet another kind of manager too, a lecherous functioning alcoholic who was a caricature of every inappropriate seventies boss that you can imagine. He would sidle up to us young girls, give us a squeeze and try and persuade us to join him in the stock room. "A slice off a cut loaf is never missed" was his catch phrase. Shocking perhaps in the context of today's culture and deeply wrong without question but it was part of the experience and in hindsight more pathetic than threatening.

This manager did no managing, he believed that his role was to lord it over us while we made the actual business work and he whiled away the long hours before his boozy lunch. No concept of encouragement, reward or teamwork, just I'm the boss, you do what you're told.

Now in my twenties, I got a job with a new entrant to the high street who were using technology to process orders to make the shopping experience more efficient and to be able to stock a wide range of goods without the floor space that had traditionally been needed. They had an enlightened approach to training and so for the first time I found that I actually enjoyed learning new skills and I relished putting them into practice. I became branch manager and learnt how to create a happy, motivated and enthusiastic team that could exceed the targets that they were set.

I moved on to become part of the regional and national management training team, developing new managers like me, helping them to understand how to get the best from people. My work was rewarding, I had status and I had job satisfaction, I had learnt that hard work and a willingness to take on new ideas could produce results that I couldn't have imagined a few years earlier.

· · ·

Over the waterfall

Although my work was satisfying it wasn't reflected in my personal life, marriage and children had revealed my husband's dark side. He'd grown up in a violent family and it became apparent that he thought that violence towards women was normal, tell-tale incidents, signposting what was to come, that had been easier not to confront at the time, escalated as his confidence grew and my dependence on him increased.

I lived on a domestic violence rollercoaster with highs when he was sorry and when I was his princess, then lows where I paid the price in blood for the everyday events that triggered his rage. I felt that I couldn't tell anyone for fear of the consequences – social, emotional and physical and so, I found myself at thirty with two young children trapped in what looked from the outside like a perfect life but was in fact a prison.

The search to understand how I had ended up with a man like this led me to counselling which I did in secret, during the day when my husband was at work. The counsellor helped me understand that I had to leave him, just for my own safety.

As the level of violence escalated over the years, I came to know that if I stuck around, my life was at risk, but more than that, counselling helped me understand that my husband's behaviour was as a result of his upbringing, so my greatest fear was of my son turning out the same. If I wanted evidence of the importance of a father's influence, I had to look no further than my kind, gentle and supportive dad, whose positive traits are reflected in all my brothers.

Without question the counsellor had saved my life, she put me in touch with a local solicitor whose daughter had been murdered by her violent partner. He was on a mission to help women facing the same threat and without cost, he helped me plan my escape, serving a restraining order on my husband once we were safely in the care of my eldest brother, many miles away.

Coming up for air

I often describe life being like rowing a boat along a river. I had been in the boat, rowing when I could, steering where I could but mainly clinging to the sides being swept down the river by the current culminating in being swept over a waterfall.

Now I came up for air and got myself back in the boat, I had survived the waterfall, but I wouldn't be able to continue my life's journey until I could find my oars.

Six months after the divorce came through, by chance, a mutual friend re-introduced me to Stewart, my first love who I'd not seen for thirteen years. He was divorced from the women that he'd left me for, we arranged to go out the next evening and (after he'd apologised) we laughed so much that we were soon seeing each other again regularly.

It wasn't all plain sailing though, my ex husband made life

as difficult for us as he could and the only thing for it was to get as far away as possible. Stewart had taken an IT contract in London and was commuting north at the weekends, staying at his flat in Islington during the week. We decided that I'd move south with the kids, we would base ourselves in the flat initially and look for a suitable family home. We spent a few weekends getting the train out of London, looking for towns where we might want to raise the children, and after stepping off the train in St Albans I realised that this was where my new home would be.

Within six months Stewart and I were living together just outside London, and my new life was beginning. Perhaps a little quicker than I had imagined, but I do believe that things happen for a reason, I had at least one oar and even if it was in circles, at least I was rowing again.

Once the kids were settled in school I realised that I couldn't only be a stay at home mum, so I went back to school. The workplace learning had given me an appetite for continuing education and even in the dark times I had done night classes, and although I don't believe that sewing and flower arranging were setting me up for a career, I had been doing something that stretched and improved me. In my new life I took on more at college, even tackling subjects that I might have thought of as too academic in the past.

There was one incident that really focussed my learning. Stewart came home from work one night, not long after we'd moved in together. I asked him how his day had been and what he'd been doing, and without really thinking, and with no malice at all, he told me that he couldn't really tell me what he'd been doing because I wouldn't understand it.

That was it. I was going to find out what he did, and learn about it, so we could have a proper conversation about his work when he got home every evening. This was back in the very early days of the first Windows operating systems, Word, Excel and Access were all very new, so I set out to learn as much about them as possible. My night classes focussed on IT and soon I had a qualification, but what was I going to do with it, other than have something to talk to Stewart about?

It turned out to be the second oar.

Setting up in business – a boat for two

This was the point when I decided I was going to set up my first business. My son was four and my daughter was at school, so I still didn't feel that I could go out and get a 9-5 job, but I needed to do something. I went to the local library as in those days they had records of all local businesses. I copied out a list of small businesses and sent them a letter telling them that they needed a database so that they could better manage their clients, and I could help them build one.

And I didn't get a single reply! Not being easily put off I rang them all up and after a few days of calling lots of local businesses, I got two appointments. To this day I'm still not sure how, but I must have sounded convincing. When

Stewart got home that evening I gave him the good news. He was a little taken aback because he had a full-time job already and wasn't sure how he would fit building databases for local businesses into that, but I persuaded him that he should take a day off work to go to the sales appointments at least. This resulted in our first customer, a fast-growing tiling business, who believed that we could build him a fantastic database that would revolutionise the way he managed his customers.

Stewart worked weekends and nights, beavering away coding databases, and then, as the business grew his brother came to join us and we converted the garage into an office. Stewart recognised that these companies would need Windows based accounts and order processing packages to operate with their databases and found a system that integrated well. I was now training people on how to use the systems, as well as selling the products.

We got ourselves noticed and a few years later we were bought by the accounts software company we were co-selling with our databases, Stewart become their development manager and I carried on my training role. It was incredible, I learned so much and got to meet some amazing people. We had sold the package to Shell Direct UK and I remember reflecting on my life's journey in the departure lounge at Heathrow, just before flying to Jersey to train the CFO on the package and discuss his financial set up, a real OMG moment!

Through all of this, Stewart was very supportive of me. If

ever I said I couldn't do something, he showed me I could, and I kept on learning. Because I was doing so much work on an accounts system I studied for the AAT accountancy qualification gaining much important knowledge about businesses and how they operate.

Eventually, the accountancy software company were sold themselves to one of Europe's biggest software houses, and I moved to the new company for a while but was ready for a different challenge. My old MD recommended me to someone in his network who was looking for an Operations Director for his software house, the first experience I had of the power of your network.

In this new role I was managing hundreds, mostly men as IT was still a very male dominated industry. I learned to trust my instincts and developed my management skills and the confidence to hold my own.

The head office was a good hour-long commute from St Albans and I was working hard, revelling in my new role but one day that all changed. My now fourteen-year-old daughter had been getting into trouble quite often at school, the school had asked me to see them urgently to discuss her behaviour and when I challenged her she told me that she was surprised that I cared because I was never there.

That bolt from the blue made me realise that my work had got between me and my family. The next day I went straight to see the Managing Director to get his help with my dilemma. He was incredibly understanding, and we worked out a way that I could progressively exit without working the whole 6-month notice period.

I realised that whatever work that I did needed to give me the time and flexibility that I wanted for my family, so I went to a high street temping agency and asked them to find me a part time admin job. The main qualification for the role that they found me was the ability to answer the phone. A start-up B2B energy company in St Albans was inundated with new customers calling in to find out why they hadn't received their contracts, so after a very brief interview, I started with them as a temp on minimum wage, something of a change from my previous senior leadership role, but it gave me the time I needed at home.

I'm capable and personable so I was easily noticed and when they discovered that I had a background in operations, process and particularly in software development they started to broaden my role, as the business grew, and we developed the software that it needed to support thousands of business customers. To do this I had to learn and understand the detail of the end to end process of energy supply, knowledge that was to stand me in good stead later in my career. The company was employing new staff like there was no tomorrow, the culture in this developing organisation was exciting and I was learning a lot about the utility industry which I came to love.

Despite my intention having been to take a back seat so I could be there for my family, I found myself in a key role developing systems and processes and managing a great well motivated team. I was working close to home and I could control the hours that I worked, which enabled me to spend time with my children.

This was a broad section of water, I had both oars in my hands, the current was helping me along and I was rowing confidently, looking back at how far I'd travelled, little did I know what was around the next bend of the river.

Sunk without a trace

Things were going brilliantly, I loved working in the exciting world of energy, and was making a real difference to the way the business operated. But my world came crashing down around my ears when I was diagnosed with cancer.

It was my son who noticed that I'd suddenly developed a double chin, and as I touched this weird swelling on my neck, I felt something pop into the bottom of my mouth. I'm not one for doctors, but Stewart made me make an appointment there and then, and at 9 am the next morning I was seeing my GP. She knew instantly that it was a tumour and by 2pm in the afternoon I was having a biopsy in the local hospital.

A week later, I got the awful news that this was a very rare type of cancer, and I needed to have an operation to remove the tumour immediately. It wasn't going to be a straightforward type of surgery. The tumour took up a significant amount of space in my lower jaw and was either attached or close to some very important structures. The doctors would have to take away a significant part of my face and neck and use a skin graft from my arm to reconstruct it, and if that wasn't bad enough, I was warned that there was a chance that I may never talk again as the tumour was resting on my vocal chords. For anyone who knows me, they can understand how awful this prospect was.

I was just numb waiting for the operation, the absolute panic that I felt, thinking about what would happen to my children if anything went wrong. Although Stewart would be devastated he would eventually meet someone else, but my children could lose their mother forever. I spiralled into it all imagining the potential outcomes, I'd not see my children grow up, go to university, or get married, it was horrific.

And then the operation itself. I woke up and every function that could be operated by a machine, was. I had a tracheotomy and a machine breathing for me. I had drains in my neck, and one from where they'd taken the skin graft from my arm. I was being fed through a tube directly into my stomach, I couldn't move, speak or do anything for myself. Those three days in ICU were the longest of my life. There was no day or night as the patients on the ward needed 24-hour care, so the hours seemed interminable. I can still hear the song the nurse used to sing as she checked on us through the night shift.

The day the consultant decided that they could remove the tracheotomy, and find out if I could speak, was almost as terrifying as the operation itself. All the doctors and nurses stood around the bed as the tube was removed, and the consultant held his hand over the hole in my throat and asked me to try and speak. The sounds that I made were indistinct and not complete words at all, but everyone laughed. It was apparent that my vocal chords were fine, but the damage that had been done to my jaw, mouth and tongue meant that it I was going to have to learn to speak again.

I'd been over the waterfall before, but this was Niagara Falls. At this moment I was under water, looking upwards through the foaming torrent at the light above wondering if I would ever surface. I had to learn to speak, eating and chewing were incredibly difficult as I'd lost all the feeling in one side of my mouth. My sense of taste had been irreparably damaged, and I often found myself choking as I forgot that I had something in my mouth, because I couldn't feel it there. I taught myself how to put food into one side of my mouth, and often had to pull things out of my throat myself when I was choking.

But it wasn't just the physical impact, there was a tremendous mental impact too. I'd had to face my mortality in a very real way, and it had changed my viewpoint on life. I had taken three months off work, but in hindsight I should have taken far longer, my heart wasn't in my work anymore and I wasn't able to make the physical commitment never mind the mental one. I left my job, and although I still worked on some projects I was ready for something different, I just didn't know what.

Lifeboat

As part of my recovery, Stewart and I took a holiday with another couple, our long-term friends. Over the course of the holiday while talking about my sense of being direction-less, the idea of starting a recruitment company was formed. My good friend Linda was an experienced recruiter and the utility sector was booming post deregula-tion. I was an industry expert so there was a massive oppor-tunity for us to work together to set up a recruitment company specialising in utilities.

This was the lifeboat that would rescue me, I just had to pull myself into it and pick up the oars.

As soon as we got back from holiday, we started to put together our plans. We based ourselves in Linda's conserva-tory and after she'd taken her children to school in the morning we'd sit down to breakfast together, and then spend the rest of the day with Linda teaching me about the recruitment industry. It wasn't too long before we realised that this idea we'd had was working, and the business started to take off. We moved into our first office, and I was pushing myself hard to learn the skills needed to succeed in recruitment, I had a lot to learn, knowing utilities was just a start point.

To build the business I'd need to have a network, but I didn't really understand the concept of networking, I'd never had to do it before. I was introduced to BNI which opened my eyes to the possibilities. I learnt a lot about networking, I found their training courses and opportunities incredibly valuable and I relished the opportunity to learn something new. I found that whilst I had never done any networking, or formal sales, I had a knack for it.

I've always been a people person, never happier than when getting to know people and building relationships, and this was how I approached recruitment. Today, I always tell my team that it's their job to know everything about their candidates, down to their inside leg measurements.

Only by really understanding the personality of the candidates and the clients can you make a good match, and that's something I am really proud of delivering on. It was important for me that we were a recruiter with a difference and one that could make a difference. Some of the early candidates I placed are now amongst my best friends, I got to know them inside out through the process and we became very close.

Fourteen years and two recessions later, Utility People is the leading recruiter in the sector working with all the big names, I have a team rowing in the same direction and I'm the cox, I look forwards and see where we are going, I set the pace and I steer the boat.

The art of recruitment is to know and understand people, their capabilities and their potential so that you can help them to progress in their career. I now know that my true passion and skill lies in working directly with people so that they can achieve their potential but creating a connection between my roles as trainer, manager and recruiter.

This has led me directly to coaching, working particularly with women in the utility industry who can benefit most from my knowledge of being a woman in a man's world. I set up my coaching business Amplify Now, so I can help people of all ages and at all stages of their career find their way, develop their confidence and discover the art of the possible.

But it doesn't stop there. Eighteen months ago, I realised that I couldn't single-handedly make a difference to all the women looking to build their careers in the utilities sector. I, along with a group of like-minded senior female leaders from the sector, set up the Women's Utilities Network (WUN), which aims to promote networking, learning and development opportunities for women across the Energy and Water sectors.

No matter what stage of their career, or what their job description, women who want to progress in Utilities are welcomed to our networking events, offered training and mentoring opportunities and given a reason to stay in the sector. WUN is now over 1,000 women strong, and with over 250 women coming along to each of our events, I am so proud of what we've achieved and excited about what the future will bring.

Gratitude, learning and self-recovery

Some people might look at my life and say that things have been hard. It's true that I have had some hard times but I'm grateful, I'm grateful for meeting that counsellor who freed me from my first husband. I'm grateful for the chance that reconnected me with my first love, Stewart. I'm grateful for the opportunities that being born into a man's world have given me, the strength to face up to difficult situations and not let men pull me down. I'm grateful for my cancer, because it made me see life differently and I'm most grateful for my wonderful family and friends, who supported me through thick and thin, and gave me courage when I needed it most.

I think gratitude is both a powerful and useful emotion and I would urge everyone to think about the things that you can be grateful for.

I encourage my colleagues and those that I coach and mentor, to think about how they can develop their skills to deal with whatever life throws at them, get back in their boat and steer it in the direction they want to go. Learning has consistently underpinned my life and work. More recently that has included NLP and coaching qualifications amongst others, as I've recognised that throughout my career I've gravitated towards supporting people to grow and develop.

Learning doesn't have to be formal education, personal growth is one of life's essentials, it helps put you in control of your life. In my opinion, if you are not learning in some way, you are going backwards and to use the river analogy again, you are letting the current take you where it goes, rather than steering your boat where you want to go.

Throughout the challenges that I've faced, I've always known that despite the support and help that I've had, ultimately, it's been up to me to be resilient and to recover myself, whether that be physically or mentally.

I have learnt that you have it within you to create the life you want, by building confidence over time to deal with the situations that life can throw at you and by nurturing the ability to pick yourself up and start again.

ABOUT THE AUTHOR

ANGELA PEART

Angela Peart is Managing Director of Utility People, the leading recruiter in the Utilities industry.

Angela has been a senior leader of people and entrepreneur for the last thirty years. Her experiences in learning and development, customer service, software development, energy supply and recruitment have built a unique skill set.

A serial entrepreneur, she now leads the energy sector's leading recruitment consultancy, and she works with people at all stages of their careers as an executive and career coach.

Angela truly values the power of her network and is in

demand as an inspiring speaker on issues such as gender equality, skills development and retention, and confidence and personal development.

Eighteen months ago, Angela recognised that more needed to be done to promote and retain women in the Utilities industry and set up the Women's Utilities Network (WUN). Now over 1,000 members strong, WUN develops and encourages women in the sector to connect with other women, so they can share learning, build confidence, and develop their own passion for the utilities space.

Angela's passion is about giving others the skills they need to succeed, in whatever role they want. She mentors and coaches individuals to develop confidence and understand their own possibilities and works with businesses in the utility space to develop their people through her coaching business AMPlify Now.

Email – angela@amplifynow.co.uk

https://utilitypeopleuk.com/

https://thewun.co.uk/

https://amplifynow.co.uk

https://www.linkedin.com/in/angelapeart/

4

CHARLOTTE LEWINGTON

Growing up I have always had the belief that my life was mapped out even before it started, almost like I was destined to be here. I believe I was sent here for a reason and that it is my mission to make a positive impact on the world. I never saw myself as being an Entrepreneur. I always believed that you had to go to school or university, get a job and work hard in order to make a living. I thought I had everything mapped out, it was always my dream to become a child psychologist.

It wasn't until I split with an ex-boyfriend and joined a network marketing company that I started to question my life. I started reading books and finding a whole new meaning of life and what it was all about. This is when everything started to change, and I discovered a different path that I was meant to be on.

It is because of my childhood and life experiences that I

believe that we cannot control everything that happens to us, but we can choose how to deal with those situations. You can either sit down and cry about things or you pick yourself up and move on, choosing to learn from those experiences and not letting them define who you are becoming.

I hope my story inspires and motivates you to know that you can do anything you put your mind to. You are here to be the change in the world you were always meant to be, so don't let anyone ever take that away from you.

My story begins with my parent's decision to not to have any more children. My parents already had three children, so my mum decided to have an operation to be sterilised. Four children meant a bigger house, a new car and needing more money which they didn't have.

Two years after the operation my mum found out that she was expecting, doctors tried to encourage her to have an abortion as they thought I would be born with a disability. I will always admire how strong my mum must have been to ignore their advice and to follow her heart even though it was extremely difficult for her to do so.

On the 10th July 1986, I was born into the world in a place called Rush Green Hospital. Nine months later, it looked as though I wouldn't survive. I was diagnosed with a serious condition known as intussusception, which happens when one part of the bowel slides into the next. It is normally boys who are more prone to getting it but for some reason this was meant to be part of my life story. I was becoming very poorly.

It was Easter Sunday and my mum decided that she wanted to have me baptised because they thought I wasn't going to survive. I was going to be taken for surgery to try and make things better. What happened next some might say wasn't just a coincidence, one of the nurses taking care of me had also been through a similar situation with her son, she persuaded the nursing team to pump my stomach one last time. It worked. Thanks to that nurse, her care, persistence and determination as well as the experience she had suffered in her own life. I was ready to carry on with my life.

On 26th June 1993, Cancer took my brother from my family when I was only six. I have lived twenty-six years without him. I have two photos next to my bed. One of all four of us, my two brothers, my sister and myself which were taken when we were younger. The other one is of my brother and me. I love those pictures. I think about him all the time and wonder what my life could have been like if It hadn't of happened, it is painful to know that I will never share my accomplishments with him, never get to celebrate birthday's or anniversaries, he won't get to see me get married or meet his nieces and nephews. I will never be able to see him again or have a conversation with him. Losing my brother changed my family's life for good.

When my brother was younger, he always seemed to be complaining of headaches and was sleeping a lot. So, my parents took him to the doctors for investigations, eventually diagnosing him with terminal cancer in particular, a brain tumour.

During this time, I remember spending a lot of time visiting hospitals and trying to make sense why my mum couldn't always give me her full attention. As a child you don't understand, you see things from a child's perspective. It is not until you grow up and look back that you realise the amazing strength and determination that both my parents and my brother had. My mum and dad not only had to cope with losing their child, but they also did their best to try and provide for their family. I grew up always being told that I was loved and wanted. Even through the bad times we went through my parents have always tried to make life as normal as possible.

Even though I was only three when my brother was diagnosed, and six when my brother died, those years have changed my life. People often say that children don't understand what is going on around them and that they are too young to understand. From my own experience plus my academic and professional training, trust me when I say children know and understand more than you realise. They may not fully understand what is going on but the most important thing to recognise is that they know that 'something is going on' and for a small child that can be a scary time for them.

I have grown to develop an understanding of how the first five years of a child's life are crucial to their social and emotional development. It is within those first five years of life that affect how a child will form attachments and friendships later on in their adult life. As well as how they develop socially i.e. self-esteem, confidence and how they perceive the world. It is these experiences that have shaped my beliefs and feelings about the world around me and are crucial to understanding where my limiting beliefs came from.

During my childhood, I remember travelling with my mum to the hospital and attending the nurseries and creches within the hospital. I only have limited memories of this time because I was very young. On one occasion whilst my brother was in hospital, I was adamant about giving my sister a kiss goodnight.

At the time we had bunk beds and I decided it would be a good idea to climb up the back and try to reach my sister, I ended up falling and hitting my head on the corner of the chest of drawers. I went running into the bathroom whilst my mum was in the bath to tell her that I had hit my head, thinking it was nothing she encouraged me to go back to bed. As I turned back around a lump of hair fell off and blood was visible, so my poor mum had to take me back up to the hospital.

On another occasion, whilst my brother was also in hospital, my dad was surprising my mum with a fortieth birthday party, I was being looked after by a close family friend. During the evening, my friend and I were playing on the stairs and my friend accidentally pushed me. I ended up falling down the stairs and hitting my head, my friend's mum brought me to my mum as she was still at the house and ended up taking me to hospital. Exactly what my mum needed on the night of her surprise party. I always did give my parents a run for their money.

With many visits to the hospital and eventually the hospice, my brother's last wish was to be able to pass at home with his family. In the last few weeks of his life, my brother was brought home to die.

During the time that my brother was ill we were supported by two charities, one was the make- -wish foundation who granted my brother the wish of meeting the Miami dolphins as this was something that he had always wanted to do. The other charity was the Rainbow trust, I remember a lady who was deeply involved with our family. She helped me learn how to ride a bike and was a tremendous support to my mum when she needed her.

I will never forget the amazing work that the Rainbow Trust did to support me and my family. I also remember the people from the church that used to make meals for us, the family friends that let us come and play with their children, the support we received was amazing and something that I will be forever grateful for.

My parents carried on with life as best as they could, however they decided to divorce shortly after my brother died. I remember always getting two holidays and the two Christmases but the pain that comes with your family being separated has always stayed with me. When I was younger, I often felt like I was supposed to choose sides, but I often refused to do that.

There are often two sides to every story and no matter what happened between my mum and dad it was between them. For years I wanted to know the truth about what happened and try to make sense of everything, but the only thing that did, was cause arguments and pain between the family.

Eventually you get to a point where you realise that no matter what has happened, they will always be your parents and whatever they did they are only human. Everyone makes mistakes. People are quick to pass judgement on others but put yourself in a similar situation and then tell me how you would react.

There is no manual or guide to becoming a parent, there is no magical way to know how to raise your children, but I know they did the best that they could with the situation they were given. I may have been a nightmare as a child, but I have grown up and I am proud of the woman I am becoming, and I am grateful to them for that.

Whilst my experiences as a child were traumatic. I am thankful I got to see and feel the real love a parent has. I witnessed the sacrifices they made and the stress they endured for the life of their child. And I am thankful for my brother, it is because of him that I learned empathy very early on in life and understand the pain of loss and loneliness.

I regret how I was as an adolescence, but since then I have

learnt that my behaviour was my way of coping with everything that I had to deal with as a child. I had lost my brother at such a young age. I was angry and not only had to grow up with the hormones of becoming a woman, I had a mixture of emotions to deal with.

It was during my school years that I believe was where my confidence and self- esteem issues began. I never believed I was pretty enough or good enough, the constant pressure to look and be a certain way always resonates with me because I never felt like I fitted in. I was never the popular girl and I didn't have many friends.

All the teachers and students at the school knew the history of my brother. A memorial garden was dedicated to him and it was amazing to know my brother made a lasting impact on everyone he met. I was proud of him, but I was constantly reminded that he was not there with me anymore.

I was suffering, I lacked confidence, I hadn't developed friendships like the other children. I worried I wasn't good enough and that I was different. Even after my mum let me change schools, I didn't fit in. The popular girls took a dislike to me and made my life hell, constantly picking arguments.

The friends I did have were the wrong type, the ones that only seemed to use me for money or for what they could get. One girl from school even went as far to mug me of my phone when I went to meet some friends. As I was walking down the train station steps, they were there waiting for me at the barriers, I tried to ignore them and go past anyway but it didn't work, and they threatened me into giving them my phone. Stupidly I did, but what else are you supposed to do when you are fearful of what they might do to you.

After finishing school. I decided to follow my passion of working with children and started at college to study a Diploma in Childcare and Education. I felt like I had made some strong friendships. There used to be a group of us that would hang out together, go out clubbing regularly together, sneak off into town for a Chinese and a have a few drinks during our lunch hour. I absolutely loved being part of a group and finally feeling like I had made friends. I had a funny relationship with one of the girls, we got on really well but then we also had our ups and downs, but no matter what happened I always valued our friendship.

One day when I was working, I received a phone call from one of the friends informing me that another friend had been killed in a car accident, I couldn't believe it. She was only a couple of minutes away from her house. I felt numb, at first, I thought she was joking as she was telling me.

A short while after I found out, I walked to the place where the accident had happened, I remember just sitting there. I wanted to know how it could have happened, why her, she had so much in her life that she was meant to do. She had decided she was going to quit the childcare course and do something else. She had met someone, and her life started to look like she was finding out what her passion was in life.

I never got to go to her funeral as my dad had booked a

family holiday that I was going on. I remember asking if I could miss the holiday to be there, but my dad had already paid for the holiday and didn't want me to miss out on going. I still paid my tribute to her whilst I was out of the country and still think about her every day.

Those were my college years. Once I had finished college and gained a Diploma in childcare, I was offered an amazing opportunity to work as a nanny in Gibraltar, this opportunity started my career working with children and is where my love for travelling began. I then went on to work in five-star resorts around the world offering a high standard of childcare to families whilst they were on holiday. I was able to gain life experience and learnt to be independent.

I travelled around the world for many years doing 'seasons', but then I decided that I should start settling down and getting my life organised. I worked with children for many years and worked my way up into management level. I then went on to work with young people in secure units which then led to me deciding to do a degree in Psychology. I loved challenging behaviour. I love the mind and understanding why people behave the way they do. I went to University in Cambridge but still continued to commute from Essex and work part time too.

A few years into my degree I met someone, he was charming and showed an interest. For the first time he was someone who made me feel special and that I was loveable. However, he was also a heavy drinker ,and had two children. He was a carpenter but lived in a small village, and the only thing that they had to do there was to go to the pub. This was one of the biggest struggles of our relationship, I didn't want to be with someone who you would always know where you would find them – in the pub! I told him how I felt, and he said he would cut down on the drinking.

For a short time, he did, and I started to love who he was. I was finally happy that I had met someone. We were always on and off and people always told me I could do better; his family didn't really like me, and I never understood why. It was so bad that his mum made it really difficult for us to see each other. We went on holiday together and just after the holiday, we split up, but after a short time we started to see each other again and it looked like we were going to get back together.

I became tired of always being on and off, I wanted him to make a decision, so I decided that I was going to move away from Essex to Cambridge because I was working and studying there, surely that would help him make up his mind as to whether or not he wanted to be with me? I should have read the signs he started to dress better, make an effort. We had been texting for a while but on the day of his birthday, I sent him a message wishing him happy birthday, I asked if he wanted to celebrate together, he made his excuses.

It wasn't until later that day that I was driving home from being at a friend's house and I had just reached my new house that the dreaded text came through. He wrote that he was sorry, but he had been seeing someone else and that it was going really well, he wished me well and hoped that I would find what it was that I was looking for. I was heart-broken, we had been together over two years and as far as I was aware, we were going to be getting back together.

How could he just end our relationship with a text? I wanted closure but I wasn't going to get it. I have no prob-lems moving on after a relationship but when you are led to believe you are going to be getting back together only to find out that they had been seeing someone the whole time, it brings up so many questions and emotions that I had to deal with. When the other person just ends it like that it doesn't allow you to have the closure that I needed.

For a long time after the break-up, it affected me badly. Even through his faults I wanted to be with him, I had accepted him for who he was and had fallen in love with him. When I reflect on the experience now, I am glad it happened. Sometimes in life we just want some closure, the hardest part of it was feeling like I had been rejected again, it made me question what was wrong with me? Why didn't he want to be with me? I know now that I was looking for love in all the wrong places. He even quoted Justin Bieber's song at me – that I should go and love myself.

As cruel as it was, he was right. I didn't love myself and I definitely deserved better than what he was bringing to the table. This experience led me to question everything about myself and my life. I realised I wasn't happy and that something had to change. I deserved better than the friends and relationships I was attracting into my life.

Shortly afterwards, I was introduced by a friend to Network marketing, it enabled me the ability to see new opportunities and a new way of living life. I know I am not alone in thinking that it is disheartening to think you can spend the majority of life, working all the time but still constantly struggling to find money to pay the next bill. Working all the hours under the sun but having very little time to enjoy the money you earn or spend time with your loved ones. .

I became tired of working all the hours under the sun and getting very little in return. The social constructs of life teach us that we are supposed to go to school, then get a job, work hard for 50-60 years and retire with very little to show for it. I am glad my eyes were opened to a new way of life and that it doesn't have to be that way.

My self-development journey began. I stopped watching television and I started attending networking events. Surrounding myself with similar people and reading lots of books on personal development, money mindset and changing my thoughts and beliefs as well as changing my routine and daily habits.

For me the network marketing opportunity was about finding out who I was as a person and what I wanted from life. The Idea of not settling for a mediocre life and knowing that I could have time and financial freedom whilst building a business from anywhere in the world really struck a cord with me. I don't have children at the moment but when I do, I want to be able to give them the best start in life and be able to show up for them when they need me.

Growing up, one of the biggest struggles I faced was having to share my mum and not being able to have the attention that I needed. Through no fault of her own, she was busy dealing with my brother, finding ways to cope and trying to bring up four children, she had to find a way to manage her time as well as go to work to get the money needed to keep us financially supported.

Growing up as a child I was selfish, I wanted my mum to be there for me the moment I needed her. Now I understand that is not always possible. However, I want to make sure that my children don't have to experience that. I want to create a life on my terms where I can provide a great life for my family. I want to be able to give back to my parents for everything they have done.

Although people say money doesn't buy you happiness, it does bring opportunities. I no longer have to worry about paying for the next bill or having a fridge full of food. Through my business I will have enough money in the bank to be able to live life on my terms and not have to settle for second best. I decided the type of people that I wanted to surround myself with and also the relationships that I deserved to have.

I have been single for over four years; I have dated in between but most of the men I attracted were the players and the commitment phobes. So, I am ok with being single because I am working on myself and who I am becoming in order to meet the right type of man, when I am ready, I will attract the right type of guy that knows how to treat a lady. A genuine gentleman is hard to find these days, but I have faith that the right man will come along when the timing is right. Just like everything else in my life has.

Through my own experiences I was able to say enough is enough, I changed my thoughts, what I believed to be true about myself, and I no longer let people that would make me feel worthless be apart of my life. I am now able to share my experiences with other women who want the same for themselves.

The online space has allowed me to create a Facebook community of women who are all striving to become a happier, healthier, better version of themselves. I wanted to create a space that allowed women to accept themselves for who they are and learn to love themselves once again. My intentions were to create a space for like-minded ambitious women who were tired of living a mediocre life and wanted more for themselves.

"The Mindset & Transformation Lounge" is a community of highly driven women from all over the world who have come together to motivate, inspire and support one another. It is within this community that women are able to come together and share their experiences and entrepreneurial journey together. It is a place that offers value and strategies to all of the amazing and inspirational women within the community.

When I reflect back on my journey of life, there are many experiences that I can pinpoint that affected my decisions, way of thinking, confidence and the ability to find happiness from within. For a long time, I was a people pleaser who did things because of the need to have validation. Coming from a place where I wanted so desperately to be liked, for people to accept me for who I am.

My purpose, my passions and my value in life to give to the world has come from the many struggles and experiences I have faced. My life has not been easy but through the challenges I faced I was able to grow and develop as a person and am able to support my clients. I had to get comfortable with being able to step out of my comfort zone and face the fear and doubt that comes with trying something new. As nothing grows within our comfort zones.

For a long time, I was scared about putting myself out there and it took me a while to become comfortable with sharing my story. I was scared of other people's judgment and worried about what they would think of me. However, once I started sharing my story people were so supportive and said how inspirational they thought I was. This meant so much to me.

In the early stages of growing my business, I was guilty of scrolling on Facebook and Instagram watching what other people were doing and wondering how they had grown their business so quickly, almost as though they had become an overnight success. I wanted that, I wanted to know the magic formula but the more I kept searching for it, the more I just remained stuck and not making much progress.

It wasn't until I stopped focusing on what every-one else was doing that I started to make progress within my own business. I found the confidence and self-belief to own my story and go out there and share it with my audience. I stopped worrying about what other people thought because it matters more about the people that I am here to serve.

If just one person believes that they are capable of more and that they don't have be stuck in a life where they are always settling for second best, then I am one step closer to achieving the desired outcome. It was time I started to own what I did and believe in myself. I began to shout it from the rooftops. It was time for me to stop apologising and start to be unapologetically who I am.

Someone once told me that it is not about me, stop focusing on myself and start focusing on what value and support I can give to my clients who are struggling with the same problems that I faced and have overcome too.

When I started becoming really clear on my mission and my vision, I was able to decide and make a commitment. When you want something badly enough you stop making excuses and you can start to take the right action to be able to get there. Once you set the intention and make a goal don't let anything distract you from reaching that end result.

In order to be able to run a successful business I needed to know the how, I invested in many coaches and learnt so much from each of them, finding the right coach has been life changing. One thing I have learned is that you have to work on yourself and your mindset first. Everything comes down to how much you believe in yourself and how open you are to seek new opportunities in order to get you to where you want and need to be.

Having a fixed mindset will only keep you stuck, but when you have a growth mindset you are open to developing and growing every single day. Having someone there that pushes you to do more and be more every single day has been amazing. For me, having someone there to make me accountable for my actions and, when I start to go off track guiding me back onto the right path, has really made a difference.

Sometimes the Entrepreneurial journey can be lonely, running an online business from behind a laptop. Being surrounded by other ambitious entrepreneurs gives you the encouragement and the realisation of what is possible. I am able to achieve exactly what I want to achieve and support other women to be able to do the same and that is so important in order to stop you feeling lonely and going insane. For the women that want to create more in their life, find other women who are going to inspire you and lift you up when you are feeling down.

Many women struggle with being able to put themselves first or being able to look after themselves without feeling guilty or selfish for wanting to do so. It is important for women to make themselves a priority, because if we start burning out this is going to show up in other areas of your life. When I was going through a bad time in my personal life I started to work more and not look after myself. It was easier for me to carry on and pretend that everything was fine.

However, one evening after working a long stint of shifts, I went home to have a bath and had really bad palpitations, I could feel my heart pounding into my back and worried something was wrong. I drove myself to the hospital and ended up getting admitted, my blood pressure was high and I knew something was wrong. This is what happens when we don't look after ourselves. Our body has a way of giving us warning signs when it is not happy. It is important for us to listen to those signs before it is too late.

I worked in a hospital I should have known better, however my experiences of working in the hospital have taught me that life is too short. I have learnt many great lessons. It only takes one minute for your life to be turned upside down. Life can change in a split second. On television at Christmas the soaps always show people's lives being turned upside down in a matter of minutes. The same principle applies working in the Emergency Department. One minute the day could be going smoothly the next minute a trauma call has gone through and there is someone coming in with life threatening injuries.

The reason why I am telling you this, is because just like

the soaps someone's life has changed in a matter of seconds. I used to see family's lives turned upside down. It teaches you to appreciate just how special life really is. It makes you understand that our lives are a gift. We have the power to make choices and decisions on what we want to do with our lives. Life is for living, we are taught from a young age to go to school study hard, get good grades, go to university, and we learn that having to work means working hard.

Life is meant to be enjoyable, it shouldn't only be about paying bills and going to work. It is time to start living life and having fun.

I am so lucky and blessed that I found a new way to experience life. I have worked on my self-worth and money mindset, I know I am worthy to set my own limits and pay rates, because I know the results that my clients have are worth their investment.

One of the reasons I wanted to become a coach is because I have the ability to listen to other people and really hear what they are saying. It is my passion and my skill that I can understand the underlying messages of what people are saying to me, I am a natural empath, I am sensitive, and I have the ability to pick up on other people's energies.

My training as a psychologist has given me the skills needed to be able to understand how the mind works and why people behave the way they do. So often people have said, I have only just met you, but I feel comfortable telling you my life story.

There is no coincidence that you have picked up this book, there will be certain lessons and blessings that you have been waiting to hear or perhaps some reassuring messages that make sense to you.

If you only take one thing from my story let it be this, when you learn to love yourself enough and just be you, the right people will fall into your life and the wrong ones will leave. When you surround yourself with the right people, those who support you and encourage you to follow your dreams, those people who build you up instead of knocking you down, you will begin to thrive.

It is down to you to set your boundaries of what you will and won't accept in your life and you can only begin to do that once you start to value and respect the woman that you are. Today I am proud to say I have grown and overcome so much over the years, every day I am working hard to grow and develop further. I no longer see my self-worth through the eyes of another person. I respect myself enough to know that the only person's opinion of me that matters is my own.

We spend so much of our lives trying to fit in to be liked and to be good enough that we forget to be our true selves and the unique contribution we have to bring to this world. For years I always tried to change who I was in order to be liked or to fit in. It wasn't until I discovered my own self development journey that I found out who I was and what it really meant to be unapologetic for who I am.

I am so passionate about helping women to realise this, and it is my mission to help other women to stop settling for second best and create a life that they love and deserve. I believe everyone deserves the opportunity to become their best self and live their best life, when you figure out how to do that it is a wonderful opportunity. I am so grateful and excited for what this year holds for my clients, my business and my life.

ABOUT THE AUTHOR

CHARLOTTE LEWINGTON

Charlotte is a Mindset & Life Transformation Coach for Female Entrepreneurs.

Her two passions in life are supporting people and making a positive impact in the world. From a young age, she always had a love for children and decided to pursue a career within the childcare profession.

After establishing an impressive career within her field, she decided to further expand her knowledge and went on to complete a Bachelor of Sciences Degree in Psychology. During this time, she discovered a passion for the mind and behaviour, and how our childhood experiences affect the way we behave as adults.

She became an expert by developing her knowledge with a Master's in Children and Young People. She began to understand how powerful the mind is, as well as how your childhood experiences affect your confidence and self-esteem as an adult.

Throughout her own childhood, she experienced many obstacles which only made her stronger, she found out from a young age that we have two choices in life, we can look at the experiences we face as happening for us or to us. She believes they happen for us. You can either sit down and cry about things or you get up and learn the lesson being shown to you.

She used these experiences to mould her into the motivational and inspiring women she is today, that is never afraid to be unapologetically herself and to support her clients to become the best versions of themselves.

Charlotte lives in Cambridge UK, and coaches' women around the globe to stop settling for second best, to become happier, healthier and the best versions of themselves, so that they can create more money and impact in a business that they love.

https://www.facebook.com/
groups/MindsettransformationLounge/

https://www.charlottelewington.co.uk

CoachingbyCharlotte@mail.com

 facebook.com/LewingtonC

 instagram.com/charlotte.lewington

5

GEMMA BOND

*E*veryone has their own inner Guru, guiding them from one place to another, totally in line with life's higher guidance; some call it god, or maybe the universe. It's that feeling when something is totally right for you and you're on the path you're supposed to be on, positive, full of growth and fulfilling. Tuning into your very own inner Guru station and being able to participate in this wondrous music is like trying to tune into let's say radio new Zealand when you live in the UK, or a DAB station when you're on analogue.

Often the harder you look the more frustrated you get trying to find it, you get distracted and lost in the generic sounds of manmade manufactured music keeping you further away from your own very unique sound. Far easier to get distracted, lost in frequencies taking me further away from the truth.

Coventry in the 80s and 90s and still today is a university of life, full of different cultures, classes and creeds in one big concrete jungle slap bang right In the middle of the country.

I always felt its lost sense of identity, not like one of the great cities of the UK, We didn't have signs for William Shakespeare's house or Robin Hood's Cave, no bridges, famous rivers or bays. We had graphitised subways with Combat 18 or National Front scribbled on the side or F**k the IRA.

Growing up as an only child with no siblings to fight my corner or feel connected to, it always seemed like an exciting but somewhat scary place to live - my home town. It was, waiting for a bus home in last year of primary school and three kids pull a knife, robbing my mate's jeans she had just bought from bay trading that afternoon.

A little later running from being mugged again on the way home from the pictures, dodging the "hard" kids in my area daily, and all the general scraps and dramas being an inner-city kid brings with it. I wanted to be an actor when I grew up, my biggest role became a game of how to hide my true nature and put on a strong front , I don't want to sound dramatic like it wasn't all "boys in the hood", I doubt anyone was going drive past our Roger's corner shop and shoot all us kids up, but I mean to stay alive emotionally , to look strong so I didn't get bullied or hurt, be dismissive of the things I really liked so I could fit in and find a way that people would respect me.

Being an only child wrapped in cotton wool it can be a lonely place so, when my friends were all busy at weekends, or my cats had run away sick of me trying dress them up as dolls, I turned to the pleasure of what was in my kitchen cupboards. Food was my best friend, my brother my sister, my short term happiness. It was my warm fuzzy place. Most kids fall asleep thinking about fairy tales, I did that too, but my fairy tales consisted of prince charming rocking up to save me with a MacDonald's, Chinese and Chips and don't forget the 10 packets of monster munch he would carry in his pocket for later, Prince charming needed some big ass pockets.

The wrapped in cotton wool life ended when my parents' marriage did. My mum re married and I rebelled, I self-harmed as I blamed myself like all kids do for their divorce. Then came the birth of my baby sister my adorable little sibling my heart swelled with love and protection like it still does today, but I felt like an outsider I didn't know where I fitted in.

My waist line expanded as fast as my confidence waved goodbye. The fat funny friend who hung around with the fittest girls in school, rebellious, popular but slightly troubled, always seeking attention from anyone that would notice me.

Often teased for being fat by boys, mostly the one waiting to walk my mate home, not very often was I the one snogging the face off whatever boy was fancying his chances with us lot that week.

Being a teenager in the 90s meant you were part of a scene, there were the Goths, townies , grunge and other fringe groups I care not to even remember now, and it was all about what music you listened to.

We were Townies that meant listening to dance, rave, indie and pop we dated football loving, Ralph Lauren, Burberry wearing lads. We completely followed the mainstream, but we strangely believed we were the kings and queens of the rebellion.

Our idols of the time were encouraging the youth of the day to get totally wasted and live your life now and not care about the future.

On my fifteen birthday this chip loving, chubby blonde kid managed to get into her first proper nightclub., As danced the night away I thought wow this is it, this is what grownups do drink bottles of Bacardi Breezer in nightclubs, party till 2 am, try to get a snog with a boy and work all day in my Saturday job to pay for the pleasure.

Bacardi Breezer was replaced cheesy nightclubs disappeared from my world, replaced with all-night raves, glow sticks, whistles, dancing for 12 hours nonstop, then the discovery of trance and house music and finally the super clubs. It was the era of the DJ and the super club, it was everywhere. I remember watching the news about fatboy slim playing Brighton beach. They expected twenty thousand people tops, to turn up that sunny day, bet security had a right good old laugh when two hundred and fifty thousand pill munching, feet stomping ravers turned up.

I can only describe to anyone who didn't live through the love dove generation, it felt like people coming together from a place of love and connection, at the time it seemed like magic. You felt like you belonged to a jilted generation of likeminded people all pushing boundaries, saying no to the establishment. We wanted to feel something, we wanted our parents battle thatcher; we didn't want to be defined into a box, go to work, live a hard working class life of mindless TV and takeaway.

Most people I know happily dipped there experimental feet into the sea of connection , adventure and uncertainty most weekends, but then one day they all sort of grew up and tuned into their inner guru station happily riding off into the sunset to create their fairy tales and dreams., For some of us I believe we didn't have a clue where to begin or what our dreams consisted off and if we did we never believed we could have them anyway, so we just sort of followed others that didn't know either and got lost, lost in something that wasn't so connected and that felt much more disconnected, and what was once the light in the darkness now filled the darkness with more shadows.

We were lost before all of this hedonism it just helped us forget, looking for the answers and the connection in all the wrong places, I'd been lost in food totally and utterly lost to the point that when I was 5 stone overweight,. I'd compared myself to my fit mates and then eat more to forget I was different and weak, this I how I saw it.

As a child I lived in my very own safe little make-believe

world, in a street that looked a bit like Coronation Street, where our two bedroom terraced home existed. I would spend most of my days in the back garden or my bedroom. A world of fairies and saving little bugs from injury outside, singing songs on my swing.

Then when I was older romantic films, and acting out being married to Patrick Swayze practicing my (later told) pretty amazing kissing skills out on his life-sized poster in my bedroom. I had no tales from my weekends, no getting up to mischief with siblings, cousins or friends like all the other kids in the areas as we didn't go to the social club or the pub. We watched TV and ate takeaway.

I found solace in my loneliness, low self-worth and sometimes troubled home life firstly in food then in drugs. It made me feel nothing but significant at the same time, respected and like I fitted in, the more I took the more I could take, just like food it became an obsession. This only child found something to belong to, a scene, and I embraced it all a little too much, I didn't take drugs like some of my feet dipping friends did, it became my life.

Then mix this with some magazine article about models making themselves sick to be beautiful and hey presto you have an 18 year old living on her own, secretly living off oranges anything else would be thrown up down the toilet, my expanding waistline finally disappeared   whilst expanding my mind in all the wrong ways.

Looking for love in all the wrong places with all the wrong people, and stacking up one after the other damaging experience after damaging experience. I was always desperate for acceptance. Pushing boundaries seeing how far I could go until someone would stop me. No one ever did.

To build anything in life, or even a good life you must have boundaries, it's a bit like building a house. You lay the foundations within those set boundaries , add brick by brick to create the walls, add a roof , windows and doors and you have a house to keep you warm, safe and cosy when the winter sets in. Some houses are built strong and last through all manner of storms , with all involved taking love, care and time over the project, it comes easy to some as they have built houses for years and pass their knowledge and boundary plans on from generation to generation.

Others houses are not as strong, less people are involved in the project, or the ones that are involved haven't been given the experience from generation to generation, and without any plans they try but alas can't lay the foundations, they guess where the boundaries are. Sometimes they get it right and lay the foundations in the right place, but other times miss the mark even if love is placed into the project it all becomes a little shaky and unstable.

Over time the walls are like a game of Jenga, about to fall down, those with strong houses don't want to come near you as you might knock their walls down with your shaky ones or damage their foundations. They don't offer to put their hard hat on and get involved as they know it's too much of a big job.

Others see your Jenga walls and want you to hold their own

shaky, no foundation walls up. Help them find their boundaries so you can stand still holding each other up, but bit by bit you realise you can't hold each other's up and it all starts to crumble until it's all rubble. Broken on the ground and no matter how much good intention you have to hold each other's up, it doesn't work it just can't, as their own foundations are not strong enough and vice a versa.

Then there are those who want to smash your walls down as they can't stand seeing the bricks and the foundations being laid. It's too painful for them as they can't seem to lay their own, and reminds them they haven't got any plans, foundations or walls so they destroy anything reminding them of this.

Foundations are built by positive reinforcement, when you first learn to lay a brick on top of a foundation, if someone tells you that's wrong, it looks stupid or it's not the right shape you will move the brick around looking for another place to lay it. You may throw the brick away all together totally embarrassed that you did it wrong and think you're better off giving up on that part of your wall and let it be a doorway instead.

You don't have the full house built so this doorway stays without a door on and for any Tom, Dick or Harry to use as they please. Or maybe you leave the glass out of your windows and sometimes it gets cold and you're not protected from feeling uncomfortable in your own skin because you don't have enough protection from the harshness of outside. You feel the cold run through your body and depending on how bad the weather is or what sort of Tom, Dick or Harry comes through your door you can get some really long-lasting damage to your wellbeing. Your house isn't protecting, or warm and cozy with you in control of who you invite in.

My walls had always been shaky, I had some foundations to start from, but the problem was I kept putting one brick up and then knock it down in the other hand. My house was half built. All through my life, I had two completely different frequencies I would tune into, One was around my personal view on my relationships with food, men and myself. I had doors and windows and one half of my house was totally unfinished I'd lay a brick then demolish it and very quickly it was derelict.

Then the second opinion of me was in my work life, my career and what I could achieve in this, again it evolved over time from various influences but always positive. I had the walls and foundations in place firmly for this half of my house and it was being furnished for a queen.

People pleasing were my thing, and in my career, this worked out great as I always got on extremely well with my managers. I would go above and beyond to get praise, which in turn made me extremely successful. When I went into to full time work at 16, I realised because I grew up in the University of Life, Coventry, I could get on with anyone. My creative imagination from acting out so many characters in my bedroom growing up as an only child helped me so much that I excelled at sales.

My confidence grew and so did my salary to the point I would walk into a new job look at the top seller and that was my minimum bar I would set myself. I wouldn't give up until I was told I was the best in the job and I knew in my heart 100% this was true in this area of my life. So much of my little self-worth came from this that no one stood a chance of beating me at sales in any job as it meant too much for me to lose. I would stare at the sales board and imagine the sales figures rising and it would happen over the next few weeks like magic the exact figure.

By the time I was 21 I was earning 60K per year, I holidayed in Mexico, I had a walk in wardrobe (well my spare room in a flat I shared with my first boyfriend at the time) I went away every weekend with the girls or my boyfriend at that time. I spent thousands on clothes and the best make up, financially I could always look after myself and then some.

But deep down I was so unhappy with who I was, I still numbed myself with drugs; ecstasy, cocaine, and weed and I looked for someone to validate that I was worth something. I battled with my weight binge eating and bulimia, I attracted some long term relationships, all of them I just fell into because they liked me and came walking through my door. I never vetted, checked or decided what I liked or wanted for my life.

Then I attracted someone who couldn't handle me trying to

lay any foundations in my life and decided to smash all the walls I had managed to place. I went from working in a financial company when we met climbing the ladder, to after 18 months together not being able to hold down a proper job, I was being mentally and physically abused within the relationship and he ripped away any little self-love I had tried to build. As nearly all my self-worth was wrapped up within my work I would do what I could which was door knocking for canvassing companies, most casual self-employed door knockers can't commit to a "proper" 9-5 for various reasons.

The energy I was around was now in the lowest demographic areas in the UK. We would start our day and go to the police station to ask which places to avoid but we would still go there, I was selling for a certain mobile phone company that wanted to enter the UK market., They had no understanding about how the UK market worked which was apparent, they didn't want the overheads of employing lots of sales staff, but wanted to flood the market so they decided to have no credit score for the handsets and contracts. So, you can imagine our sales pitch suited these areas and was a bit like, "do you want a free phone?" and people were amazed when we said no credit score.

During this time something happened, I was an expert at mirroring customers, I tuned into completely different energy frequencies 60% of the people we had been selling to, didn't work and had drink and drug issues and the same with the people I was canvassing with. I found myself not turning up for the days canvassing up and down the country, but instead going down the job centre for crisis loans and sitting in parks with drunks and drug addicts with my then so-called boyfriend.

Energy is like a magnet it clings onto whatever is around it. Like attracts like , The more time you spend replicating an energy force the more you will become it. I watched a programme once about a rising star in television journalism, he had decided to do a fly on the wall documentary about heroin addiction, and he filmed addicts over six months. The documentary I watched was 10 years later after he had started his filming; they had gone back to him as he was now a heroin addict and trying to get clean. He had taken heroin to film his reaction but then became just like the people he had been filming, addicted.

If you have strong foundations and good walls then maybe you could spend periods of time within certain frequencies and you're more protected so you can walk away with your own frequency intact and pretty unaffected. But say you have no walls or you have doors and windows where walls should be then that outside frequency is going to come seeping in through those gaps until the frequencies match and you feel some sort of connection and your own unique inner Guru frequency is completely drowned out by the manmade ones that we are so easily distracted by.

I never went as far as heroin or crack cocaine, but I was using food and other drugs to numb my pain of being totally disconnected to myself. One day I walked into a church I sat praying for help, crying, the priest sat by me and asked me "are you ok?". I answered, "is god real, will he hear me if I ask for help" the priest in his soft kind voice answered, "yes if you're honest , if you're truthful, he will". I walked up to the alter knelt down on my knees and cried with my head in my hands muttering through my tears over and over "please help please give me the strength to see a better day".

Over next 12 months twice I failed at attempts of suicide, I'll be honest I never wanted to end my life, I could never be so selfish to leave my little sis with no big sis, it was more a cry for help. For someone to pick me up and take me away somewhere safe, every time I sat alone sobbing and finally had the guts to take a pack of pills, I would be sick straight after as I was so scared but being awake in this life also seemed so much more frightening. I continually made excuses to the crisis team and the police for the behaviour.

Where was the girl that had swam with dolphins in Mexico? I would ask myself, I had been the top seller with the popular friends. Then one day something snapped after being called fat in public and humiliated within my relationship I joined the gym, secretly. I had gained 3 stone in weight but instead of binge eating and smoking cannabis. I ran every other day for 3 months whilst staring at music videos on screens visualising myself having that body, and the weight dropped off me, by exercising I was changing the structure of my brain and I started to believe in me again.

My mum knew i was in trouble, she helped me pass my

driving test and I got me a little car from a friend of hers. I got a new job in sales for an energy consultancy firm. When I was thrown out of the flat onto the streets at 1am by my boyfriend I would just sleep in my car. As I regained control of my life, he started to lose control of his and started taking crack cocaine. I left on the day I found out, it was lower than my inner morals could take I wasn't willing to be with someone who was that damaged or who could damage me anymore.

Partying drugs were one thing but crack cocaine was on another level. It took four months until I didn't have to look over my shoulder; I slept on people's floors to be safe away from where he could find me. When I went to places I knew he might be I would honestly be frightened for my life. Then one day he was sectioned trying to break into one of my friends' houses looking for me and he finally left me alone.

I had to rebuild but also find the boundaries and foundations I never had in the first place. Towards the end of my 28th year on this planet I managed to get things together a little more. I joined a drama group so I could be around better energy and follow a little bit of my inner guru calling. I had been in my job a couple of years, I got a promotion, I was earning good money again, and I rented a house and decorated it just how I liked it, I rented a room to a mate and owned two cuddly pet rabbits called Walker and Winnie.

I was rebuilding brick by brick but still had way too many

windows and doors in my fragile structure. I took much less than I deserved with relationships, always being taken advantage of because of my good nature, laying one brick and still blowing it up soon after, leaving me more frustrated and loosing hope in my ability to build anything long lasting and strong.

I still drowned my sorrows in drugs which had now taken the form over past 6 years as extreme cannabis use, totalling to a habit of nearly 10k per year, I could have bloody brought a house let alone build one excuse the pun.

Then something I never expected, happened, my family told me that my dad who had brought me up for 28 years wasn't my real father.

The anger I held inside was intense, I choose to meet my real father and it was awful. The pain of being lied to and not ever knowing who I really was, hit me so hard, it was the worst but in way I can now say also the best thing, that had happened to me. Finally, it all made sense I finally knew who I was but still seemed so confusing, my drug taking increased, I went back to partying all night, rarely going home only to feed my pets. I'd Leave work and go straight out, being totally wild staying up till stupid o'clock in the morning. Work turned a blind eye to my lateness and increased sickness. In the end I got arrested three times in three years, once for affray, second for possession of drugs and third drink driving. My life was spiralling out of control. Something had to change.

One of my friends sat me down and showed me a DVD called the secret, and it blew my mind.

I watched the secret over and over again, I knew in my heart the secret made complete sense and the "law of attraction" was real. I watched my friends manifest good relationships and everything they had ever wanted all because they believed it was possible for them and vice a versa, I watched friends create nothing of what they wanted at all because that's what they believed.

I made gratitude lists; I made vision boards I wrote out my goals as I already had them. I visualised my own business, my own home I had bought, a beautiful relationship, living in a beautiful place and me being clean and healthy, happy and strong.

Don't get me wrong I still had lots of limiting beliefs around this entirely. But I knew that half of my house had been built with strong boundaries, foundations and walls, the career side of my life. No one, including myself could ever understand how I could be so highly functioning in one area of my life but a total wreck in the other. Now I knew it was me that had created it all and all I had to do change my mind set, my environment and take control and create what I wanted. Build that house Fit some doors, glass for my windows and then hopefully keep out the frequencies of things that don't serve me and find my own inner frequency my inner Guru and finally follow this.

But how, I now had the secret of how to build it but I knew I couldn't do this alone.

I went to hypnotherapy, I attended workshops, things like looking at the inner critic within you, at the time I didn't think any of it was working and I was still going ten steps forward and five back. I can now see you can look at a building being built and it still looks like a building site then one day you walk past and it's finished, you never walk past before its finished and think wow that's nearly done, it will look great when it has that final bit of scaffolding taken down.

Over a period of time, the little things you do are the most important that make a house a home. I was doing all this great self-development work, but still doing drugs daily. I was dipping my toe but not fully immersing myself as I still had so many distractions around me.

I went to train a new start-up company in Newcastle with work; I decided it would be good for me to take the week in Newcastle as a mini detox. I could go to the gym, swim and eat healthy. Instead, I ordered chips from room service then with the guilt made myself sick, and then I would drink a bottle or two of wine to block that out. By the fourth night, I was curled up on the floor in the bathroom crying. I just couldn't keep being self-destructive like this anymore, just before any major breakthrough you have one hell of a major breakdown and this was it.

I cried, but not just any cry, when your soul sobs, I was 32 years old, and I was so far away from the person I wanted to be. I was starting to lose hope, I just didn't want to carry on with this addictive pattern of self-destructive behaviour, I asked god for a break.

The next day I was completing my last day of training, as I said my goodbyes they decided to ask me if I would like to help build the business. I knew 100% I could do it, and after I could then use the money I received to build my own business in my passion.

I needed to get off cannabis and stop using cocaine occasionally before I moved. I found an addiction counsellor, he told me to go to narcotics anonymous, but I couldn't accept I was an addict, I attended the NHS addiction clinic 5 years earlier and had found myself totally out of place with crack and heroin addicts and the lady telling me that cannabis wasn't addictive. So I just believed it was a flaw in me I needed to fix.

But after 3 months of trying and failing by myself, the move to Newcastle and the new job looming, I went. I sat outside my first meeting crying, feeling sick, I had to go in. When I left a weight lifted off my shoulders I met someone who also had cannabis addiction. As he shared his story I found a sense of relief that I wasn't alone in this struggle. I took what I needed from NA I never followed all the 12 steps as I didn't need to. I found my own journey of self-development that would lead me down similar practices anyway, they insist that every time you attend a meeting you stand up or sit and say, "my name is Gemma I am an addict".

I knew the more I kept affirming this to myself and the

more I put that out to the universe the more I would be affirming this as my current state, I think NA is great and really works for some people and without it I don't know where I would be now. It meant when I moved I was ready and had more skills in my tool bag to cope with whatever was coming my way; the move wasn't easy even though it was exciting I quickly learned that energy follows you. If you have always listened to a certain radio station your auto tuner still reverts to this, the sound might not be as clear but it's still there until you physically find another one to tune into.

I found weed in a teapot under the sink in my new flat I had moved into. I flushed it down the toilet. I volunteered in two different places to make friends, both places everyone went outside and smoked weed. I never went back. I was bullied by two staff members in my new job; they put fish down my chair and all over my desk but denied it. I didn't fight back I just focused on doing a better job than them and they were fired.

I completely shifted my energy elsewhere, I painted, took long walks, read self-development books, attended workshops and seminars in self-help and mindset, I learned to love myself, and I finally tuned into my inner Guru. I took things that had happened to me and I wrote them down and then ripped them up or burnt them, I wrote a letter to my real father I never sent it, but I forgave him. I took long baths to nourish my body something I always loved to do but never kept it up, I did juice cleanses, learned more about nutrition. I decided who I would make friends with, who would be the truest reflection of me and good for my soul.

I dated and enjoyed it as I was in control to go on another date, I listened to my inner Guru even if there seemed to be chemistry, I would look and think is this person good for me long term. I wrote my goals down and still, I made gratitude lists and thanked God every day for that break.

Over a 6 year period the goals I had written down in the first year started to come true. I wrote that I wanted to buy an apartment overlooking the river with a balcony so I could listen to the birds. I wanted a nearly new white convertible car, I wanted a relationship with a man whose morals matched my own, I wanted the business I moved away to set up to be making so much a month, and I am part owner and have shares. I wrote that I then wanted my own separate business in wellness and self-development, and work from home and I wanted to get married.

I sit here now typing in my office at home, in my apartment I have lived in for three years that overlooks the river (well a whole marina with boats and everything). Where I can often hear the birds, I have a white convertible that was 2 years old when I got it, I met a man who I knew from our first date I would marry, who is the most honest caring patient and loving man, who I will marry next year in a garden abroad. The business I set up I part own and have shares in, now brings in enough money for me to start my business in wellness and self-improvement one day a week, and I am Vlogging my journey as I build this.

I have and still continue to build my house, find my boundaries, lay my foundations and brick by brick build those walls to keep me safe, nurtured and happy. So I can sit and tune into my inner guru. But I can say I am tuned in a lot more than ever before and it feels so amazing that I want others to experience this.

My wellness business Bring Out The Guru will be a hub for people, events and material I feel will help people rebuild themselves so they can too tune into their own inner Guru and create the life they truly deserve while I Vlog my own journey through this.

Then there is the dancing, I still love to dance and party but minus the hangover (most of the time) and I recently travelled to London for what I can only describe as a conscious party, one big nightclub full of people drinking health drinks and dancing the night away it was amazing and I want to bring that to the nation also, alcohol free, guilt and hangover free parties without the enhancers.

But the oldest door still open is food, I no longer binge and make myself sick, but I do still crave things that no longer serve me, and I really want to understand why so I can help others with food addiction. Like any addiction we are doing it to serve us with pleasure, safety and security. I will be a trained food Psychology coach by the end of the year, I don't believe in diets as they don't work, we need to change the landscape of our thoughts and I am the Guinea pig for this groundbreaking work, so I can help others tune into connecting their mind body and soul through eating consciously.

I Bring Out The Guru in me one day at a time, and want others to know that they can find it too and tune in to the sweetest sounds directing them to a more purposeful and authentic life.

ABOUT THE AUTHOR

GEMMA BOND

Gemma Bond was born in Coventry growing up in the heart of the inner city. As a child she describes herself as The Florence nightingale of insects and small creatures until her teen-self found other distractions in the form of Clubs, Pubs and late night antics.

Gemma has overcome adversity while managing to create great success in her 24 year sales career. Co-Founding Telex UK an energy consultancy for UK business with a difference to truly serve the client with honesty and clarity, while she remains mostly still working within the more corporate side of her businesses, she is now leading with her heart and is in the process of creating a space for her voice to be heard. To empower other women overcome similar situations she has faced, to find their Inner Guru and create the life they desire.

Vlogger of her own journey on finding and keeping in tune with her Inner Guru, Trainee food psychology coach, and Founder of The Homeless Project NE.

Her mission is to build the UKs first Self-Discovery Agency "Bring Out The Guru" to bring out Gurus, Events and Material all in the field of self-discovery and empowerment so people can live a more fulfilled, purpose lead, authentic life and truly bring the guru out in them.

Email – Bringouttheguru@gmail.com

facebook.com/bringouttheguru

youtube.com/bringouttheguru

6

GEMMA EVANS

*W*hat is my other option?

When life knocks us down, we have 2 options right? Stay down or get back up. For me there was no other option so when people asked me "how do you do it, how do you keep on getting back up?" My reply was always simple, "What is my other option?"

I'm Gemma, I'm a mam to 2 little boys Strand and Davis – without them I would have allowed myself to have 2 options, to choose to stay down or get back up, everything I have ever done is for them both. I'm a partner to Gary, thank you for showing me love, even when I sometimes made it impossible for you to be around me, let alone love me. I'm also a mammy to my fur baby Riio, You completed our little family Riio, thank you for giving me the chance to be your mammy and prove myself.

I believe that God gives his hardest of battles to his toughest of warriors. I believe I am one of his warriors. My journey through life has made me strong, strong enough to redis-cover who I am as a person, to help me rebuild myself mentally, physically, emotionally and spiritually, my strength gives me the ability to help other people rebuild themselves and do the same.

Let me share my story with you.

From as far back as I can remember my dad was ill. He would have mood swings, he would shout at us for the smallest of things, he would go to bed for days on end, meaning we wouldn't be allowed to make the smallest of noise. I can only ever recall him telling me he loved me once, just once. He found it hard to show his emotions and we would often not know what type of mood he was in which meant we constantly walked on egg shells and we only ever expressed our feelings if given permission.

It wasn't until I was older did I realise he had depression, if I'm honest I didn't really know what depression was. I just knew what it made us feel like as a family. I loved my dad, he was my hero, the man I looked up too, so it broke my heart the night I realised just how bad his depression was.

I would have been 9 or 10, my mam woke me from sleep-ing, "Gemma, come with me I need your help". Sleepily I followed her into the living room, confused and still half asleep I didn't know what was going on and then I saw him, lying on the settee, eyes rolling not making much sense. I looked to my mam for answers, guidance, anything? She just looked back at me with tears in her eyes, I could see she was just as frightened as me, so I asked her what was wrong with him. He has taken too many tablets with lots of alcohol" was her reply, "an overdose".

I gave him a cuddle and I remember thinking that this was the man who should have been caring for me, not the opposite way around. I can't remember how long I stayed up with him and my mam for, I'm not sure if I have blocked it out on purpose or I have forgotten because I spent years trying to forget about it. I do know that after that night I knew that I must be strong. Strong for him, strong for my mam, strong for my sister and strong for my brother and I must not, under any circumstances show my emotions, showing my emotions would make me weak.

So that's what I did, my dad would always say that crying meant you were weak and so I adopted that attitude too, I became a little girl who, under no circumstances would show her emotions and trust someone? You've got to be joking me, if you trust you got hurt! I trusted my Dad, look what he had done.

The image of my dad on the sofa that night will be with me until the day I die, its an image that will stay with me forever.

My Dad was placed in a mental hospital not long after that, my Mam told people that he was working away, but i knew the truth. He was there for about 4 weeks I think but I honestly don't know, I've never asked my Mam, I just know it felt like forever. When he came home, I thought things would be normal again, and they were for a while, but it wasn't long before the familiar walking on eggshells or silences began again.

I do know that in the years that followed my Dad tried several times to take his life, each time he was found or was unsuccessful. It just became the norm for me, i never spoke about it with my Mam, she didn't need my questions on top of everything and as for my sister and brother, they were too young to be worried with it, so I just kept it to myself.

When I was 13 years old, we moved back to the place I had grown up, we had lived in Bedlington, Northumberland for 4-5 years and I'd missed the place I called home like mad.

My Grandparents where there along with all the family, my Dad even started working in a local factory and was soon promoted to an engineer. My parents were "Showmen" you see, so I grew up on the fairground, each week waking up in a different place. I loved it and was often the envy of all the other kids at school because I only attended 6 months of the year, and the rest of the time I would be sent work to do from the travelling teacher.

It wasn't like it is now, and I never really did my homework. I had all the education I needed, learning the way of life, visiting new places, handling money and learning customer service skills every day. We bought a house and moved out of the caravan that we lived in, although it was a massive change for us, a stable job and home would make my Dad better right?

It was 20th November I was 17yrs old. I was off work; my

Mam and Dad had recently split up and I took some time off as the events around the situation were hard and took us all by surprise. My sister was off school too as she was ill that day, it started in the morning, Mam coming in my room about 7.30am to tell me that my Dad had walked out of work and didn't tell anyone where he was going, because of the events that had happened over the last couple of weeks I didn't think much of it, sleepily I told my mam not to worry and turned over and dozed back off.

1.30 there was a knock on the door I answered it, expecting it to be a parcel or sales person but 2 Policemen where stood there, asking could they speak to my mam I called her to the door, and she invited them in. They asked if there was somewhere, they could go to speak to her alone and she took them into the living room, I didn't need to be told what had happened I just remember her screaming as I walked in and the police were trying to comfort her.

My Dad had been found a short distance from our house by a man walking his dog he was in his car with a pipe leading from the exhaust into the driver side window, he had blocked the gaps with clothes that he had in the car. He had been found dead. My Dad had killed himself.

My mam immediately wanted her own mam and as she was comforted by my Grandma, I tried to soothe my sister, that's when it hit me. My Brother was still at school he had no idea, I needed to go to him. The police offered to give me a lift and with my Grandma by my side I made my way, in the back of a police car to the school. I had only left the same school 18 months earlier, as we pulled up in the car park it hit me what I was about to do.

We were taken up to the head masters office and as I waited, I remember looking around the room. I had never been in here before. The door opened and there stood my brother, I could see he was surprised to see us and thinking back I think he probably thought he had been caught doing something he shouldn't and was about to receive a telling off. If only that was the case. I invited him to sit on my knee and with a massive deep breath I held back my tears and told him.

I broke my brothers' heart that day and his little face will haunt me forever, I can say that it was and still is one of the hardest things I have done, ever. Seeing his little face crumble broke my heart, his Dad, his hero, the man he looked up to, the man who was supposed to be his role model was gone forever.

The police took us all home, we returned to a house full of family and friends, I remember I wanted to scream but I didn't, I needed to be strong right now, stronger than I had ever been.

The next few weeks passed in a blur and I don't remember much. I helped with the funeral planning, the insurance policies, and all the things a family must deal with when a loved one passes. I do remember this though: the bond I created with my brother became unbreakable. And it still is.

I went through the motions of grieving and in true 'Gemma-style' I made sure that everyone else was okay, often neglecting my own feelings. I became so angry with my dad: how could he leave us? We were his children! He didn't even leave us a note. A parent always puts their children first, right? It wasn't until I held my firstborn on my chest for the first time nearly eight years later, that I truly understood how bad my dad's illness must have been.

I remember looking down at this beautiful baby boy and I instantly hated myself for hating my dad for leaving us. For years I'd blamed him, and now I realised that it was an illness, and no matter how hard he tried to fight it, it wouldn't go away. I remember our family priest talking to us and likening depression and mental illness to cancer; he said that sometimes, no matter how hard we try to fight it, or how much medication we take, it doesn't work, and the illness wins. I'd never thought about depression in this way before.

When my second baby was born twenty-one months later, as I held him for the first time, I again apologised to my dad for not understanding his reasons for leaving us.

Life with two small babies was hard. My husband worked away and I often survived on coffee alone, but it was so rewarding, and I had support from his parents. I loved every minute of it. Life was good. My health visitor kept a close eye on me as she knew about my dad from my medical history. "I know what to look out for," I told her. "Post-natal depression won't happen to me; I know the signs."

Four weeks later, on a Sunday afternoon, my mobile rang. "Hello?" I answered. As the person on the other end spoke, my world stopped. I battled to make sense of what they were saying.

My brother. Car crash. Critical. Theatre. Might not survive. Hand badly hurt.

I was with my uncle and I passed the phone to him. He took the message, then came off the phone and told me that my brother had been in a serious car accident and was currently in the RVI (Royal Victoria Infirmary) in Newcastle. He was being taken down to theatre at that minute and they couldn't tell us anymore. My mam had rushed to be with him.

We waited for what felt like forever. Hours passed, then finally a phone call. It was my mam's husband who was with her at the hospital. They'd saved my brother's life, but he was in a bad way. They hadn't been able to save his right arm and it had been amputated at the elbow. I dropped the phone and sank to the floor. My baby brother, I had done so much to protect him since my dad died. How could this have happened?

"Snap out of it Gemma!" a voice inside my head told me. "This isn't about you, it's about him". He had recently married, had a young baby of his own and a very good career as an electrician. So, again i did what I know best and I put all my energy into him and everyone else. When the hospital made an appointment for a counsellor to see him a few days later, he asked my mam and I to be there too.

The counsellor spoke first with my brother, and then his wife and my mam took it in turns to ask questions. All I remember doing was holding back my screams. I remember telling him that i felt like my brother had died, he said that was normal as actually a part of him had died, we would never see that part (his arm) of his body again. "Its quite normal to feel like that too" he said.

That night in bed I couldn't get my head around the fact that he was still here, but his arm was gone. I was grieving ... and he was still alive. I sobbed myself to sleep that night, my husband was in bed next to me, but he might as well have been in another country as I didn't let him comfort me. In fact, I let him nowhere near me. I was woken by the sound of my baby crying next to me in his Moses basket. It was morning, and no matter how much I wanted to stay in bed and cry, I had two little boys who needed me.

The next few weeks passed in a blur of nappies and feeds, my husband went back away to work, and it wasn't until my aunty visited that she made me realise there was something wrong with me. I hadn't washed my face or brushed my teeth or hair in days; my curtains were closed, and the house was silent apart from the kids' crying or gurgling. I wasn't even sure when I'd last eaten. She called my mam and my husband's mother and they took me to see the local doctor.

His words might as well have been put in an envelope and

posted to the other side of the world: I'd no idea what he was saying! I couldn't concentrate, my head was full. But full of what? It didn't make sense; I didn't even know how to talk; my words just wouldn't come out.

I later understood that I'd suffered a mental breakdown. I was so embarrassed. How could this be happening to me? After everything I'd been through with my dad, I should have seen it creeping up on me, I should have done more to keep it at bay.

Soon after I asked my husband to leave our home. He'd done nothing wrong; I'd just fallen out of love with him. They say in life you either grow together or you grow apart, and we had grown apart. Nothing much changed for me and life carried on as normal as I set about being a single mother.

We'd been separated for nearly eight months when I got talking to someone on social media, a local man who'd moved back to our village after separating from his wife. We had mutual friends and he seemed a nice, genuine guy. When he asked me out on a date, I felt I had nothing to lose.

He invited me to his home for a cup of coffee. It was a beautiful summer's day and we sat in his garden and chatted. He only lived half a mile from my house, next door to one of my old school friends, so I felt safe. I noticed that he was extremely interested in my life and my friends. He commented that I was liked by everyone in my local pub, which was now his local too. I did find it odd that he made these remarks, but never once thought they were anything other than friendly 'chit chat'. I felt my ex-husband had who had worked away never really paid me much attention, so I was a bit flattered if I'm honest.

He walked me home and I remember feeling those little butterflies in my stomach as he kissed me goodbye. That night I went to bed with a warm fuzzy feeling inside. We texted back and forth over the next few days and seemed to have a lot in common. I was due to go on a night out with my friends and said I'd text or call him the next day. Looking at my phone half way through the night, I realised I had more than six texts from him. 'Bless him,' I thought as I messaged him back.

Things moved quite quickly after that: I was showered with love and attention. He would turn up to my house after he'd been on a night out or would invite me back to his. On one occasion he commented that he just wanted to see how I was dressed. Once again, I found it flattering as it wasn't something my ex-husband would have noticed.

It was about six months later when I first realised that something wasn't quite right. I was handing my car keys back to the finance company as my partner had said it was silly paying for 2 cars and I could just use his when I wanted, as I had always been careful with money it made sense, but as I was handing the keys back it suddenly hit me. Every time I had to speak to my ex-husband about the house or our joint debts, it would cause an argument. Apparently, I was spending all my time talking to him.

Maybe I am, I thought to myself. I wouldn't like it if the shoe was on the other foot, so I need to be more considerate.

I declared myself bankrupt to minimise contact with my ex and handed the house back to him. I had a roof over my head with my boyfriend and he was providing for me, so why did I need a house with my ex-husband? I reduced the hours I worked in my spray tanning business as this 'ate into OUR time'. Eventually my business, which seemed to cause arguments too, folded. In the end I even re-homed my two adored little dogs to please him. I no longer recognised the person I had become. My car was the last thing to go.

One night, after another argument and me being accused of not putting his feelings first one thing led to another and I tried to leave. He hated that I dare to even consider it and he dragged me from the back door to the bottom of the stairs. I fought back as he tried to carry me up, but too sore and tired, I eventually gave up. He pushed me onto the bed and pulled at my dress to make sure I got into bed and stayed there. I resisted and managed to flee the house.

I turned up at my brother's house. I didn't even need to say what had happened; they just took me in, made me a cup of tea and gave me a bed. I didn't sleep much that night. My head was spinning. What had just happened? How had it happened?

My phone never stopped pinging with messages telling me he was sorry and that if I hadn't tried to leave it wouldn't have happened, if I hadn't of made him feel that way it wouldn't have happened. Once again, I doubted myself and wondered if it was in fact all my fault.

The next day I got a lift to his house to collect some things for me and my two boys, who'd been at their dad's the night before. As I opened the door I was shocked to see his mother standing there. "You've given my son a black eye!" she told me. I was in disbelief and couldn't speak so I lifted my dress to show her the black and blue bruises down my left-hand side, starting from the top of my ribs and ending half way down the top of my leg. I also pointed out the ripped bra I was still wearing, a result of him trying to rip it off me to force me to stay in the house.

"These things never happened with his wife!" she told me. I left feeling confused. Had this all been my fault?

My family and friends told me how much they'd been worried about me, and how much I had changed as a person. I'd had no idea. He'd only raised his hand to me once. I'd always felt I could handle him.

With the help of my brother and grandma, I rented a house. I had nothing at all and my grandma (God rest her soul) gave me three knives, three forks and three spoons. I used to walk round to the local shop every morning and buy fresh ice and milk. I didn't have a fridge, you see, and it was the middle of summer, so I'd pour the ice into the centre of the sink to keep the milk fresh for the kids' cereal every morning. I'd walk them both to school and call in at my grandmas on the way home so I could use her washing machine. My friend had given me a corner sofa and I slept on that. The only room in the house that was decorated was the boys' room.

Around the same time a friend texted me to say that the company her mother worked for was recruiting for Area Managers. She wanted to put my name forward. I agreed and four days later I went for an interview. Next day I received the call to say I had the job. I was able to start immediately, and they arranged for my company car to be delivered the following week. I honestly couldn't believe it! With my first wage I bought a fridge-freezer, washing machine and treated myself to a night out with the girls, my first night with my friends in months.

I was still getting text messages and phone calls all day and all night, begging me to take him back. I was exhausted, but I knew a night out would do me good. Half way through the evening I looked up and there he was, standing across the dance floor staring at me. I froze.

We moved pubs but he followed us to the next two. I was pleased when it was time to go home and tried to ignore the constant phone calls I was receiving from him. My friends dropped me off and I got into bed. I remembered a conversation I'd had with his sister a month before as we walked our dogs: she'd told me that when they'd argued in the past, he'd phone her and threatened to kill himself. I decided to turn my phone off.

The next morning, I woke up and immediately turned my phone back on to check if my boys were okay at their dads and what time they would be home. As it was loading up, I could see there were over fifty missed calls, numerous text messages and a video message. I clicked on the video and my heart stopped. He was sat on the floor of his living room slitting his wrists! There was blood everywhere: up the walls, in pools on the floor and all over him. He was telling me I had caused him to do it as I'd ended our relationship and was making a new life without him.

Jumping up, I called an ambulance and then his parents. By the time I got to his house, his parents, the paramedics and police had already arrived and were treating him. He had told his parents that I had taken another man home and that's why he had done it, his dad came out and threatened me, the police officer was awful to me and said some horrible things, she told me to leave. I walked away with the voice in my head telling me that it *was* my fault. If I'd just given him a second chance, he might not have hurt himself so badly. I couldn't save my dad from his mental illness but maybe I could save this man.

He called me the next day from his hospital bed and I agreed that I would give him a second chance if I could save him then I would and that's what I was going to do.

Over the next seven months things went from bad to worse and I soon realised that I'd made a mistake taking him back. I walked on eggshells. Every time I said or did anything he didn't like, he threatened suicide. I became a person even I didn't recognise again, lashing out and doing what I could to survive, I drank loads and was violent to anyone who stood in my way.

On December 27th, 2013, he had been out and had been drinking all day, when he returned, he tried to strangle me. The police were called, and he told them we'd just had an argument. They pointed to the marks around my neck and the officer told him that it didn't look like "just an argument"! He was arrested and given bail; his phone confiscated. I was put on first response by the police and had a panic alarm fitted.

I was visited by an organisation for victims of domestic abuse, and they explained to me that this was the type of relationship I'd been in. I'd no idea what they were talking about and explained that it was only the second time he'd raised his hand to me.

On New Year's Eve I got the call to say that he'd tried to kill himself again by driving his car off the road, and he was back in hospital. I booked an appointment with the police and asked them to drop the charges. I believed he needed medical help for a mental disorder and prison wouldn't help him. What I was told in response hit me like a ton of bricks.

"On the night of December 27th, we received a call out and my officers got to your address in rapid time. They had no idea, because of the screams that could be heard through the control panel, what they would be met with, and for that reason the CPS has decided to go ahead with the charges, with or without your backing. Gemma, we believe that you're a victim of one of the worst cases of domestic abuse we've seen for a long time'".

I left the police station in a daze.

Although he was bailed to his parents address nothing much changed. He'd turn up at my house during the night, cold and dirty, saying he was sleeping in his car as he couldn't stand to be at his parents. I had no idea if it was true or not, but I couldn't bear to see him in this state. I was trying to protect him and too blind to see what it was doing to me in the process.

We went out for a couple of drinks for Valentine's day, while my boys were staying at their gran and grandad's. I did everything I could to try to keep things from kicking off or escalating, but when we returned home late that evening, things turned very nasty. I don't remember how I got there, but I was pinned on the kitchen floor, him sitting on top of me with a knife to my throat. I tried to move it away and it cut into my hand. He was spitting at me, hitting me on the head with the knife. I tried to fight back but it was no use, he was too strong. He was shouting that it was my fault, he was going to kill me, and my boys would grow up without a mother.

Hearing him talk about my kids growing up without me triggered something inside of me, I have no idea where I got the strength from, but I kicked him off and made for the living-room to get my panic alarm. It was gone! He had moved it! The box that controlled it was under my bed and I knew I had to get there. I ran upstairs, i remember tripping on my way. It was as if things were moving in slow motion. I got under the bed and pressed the button. I could hear him coming and my life flashed before me.

I remembered the words of the policeman about not knowing what they were coming to the last time they were called out, a domestic or murder scene. This time, I thought to myself, they're coming to the scene of a murder. Each foot step that he made up the stairs seemed to ring in my ears. As he reached my bedroom door the dialling tone on the alarm sounded. I knew help was on its way.

He heard the sound too. He picked up my phone and fled. Then he texted all his family, pretending to be me, telling them we had an argument and that this time he really was going to kill himself. The police arrived, searched my house and put me in a safe place for the night.

"You bitch! They'll lock me away for this!" he said to me as he fled. They were the last words I ever heard him say. The next day I was advised that he had taken his own life.

The last five years have been hard. I have had to mentally, physically, emotionally and spiritually repair myself. I've often felt like giving up. But then I remember the pain that my dad caused when he gave up. I will never put my children through that pain.

I am now an ambassador for domestic violence, a motivational speaker and I help women learn about self-love. I teach them how to fall madly in love with themselves through my Warrior Women Academy and my Women Who Can mentorship.

I had no idea what coercive control was or that it even existed for that matter. I thought domestic violence was a hit a punch or a slap, I thought it left a mark on the skin. I sometimes wonder to myself if that would have been easier to understand, if i had a bruise or a cut then would I have gotten out before I did? I wonder that if he hadn't of taken his own life what would have happened to me? Would he eventually have taken mine?

It took me a long time to be able to tell my story in full, even the version that I have told you today is so condensed, I will eventually write my own book but for now I am happy with a chapter.

Telling my story about what happened to me still doesn't seem real, I feel like I'm reading the story of someone else, and yes, I do ask myself what I stayed for? Why didn't I see what he was doing? The truth is, I was so worn down from it that I used to question it in my head. I did think I was mad at one point.

Domestic abuse affects thousands of women, and men every year. If I can save just 1 person by telling my story then it will have been worth it.

If you are reading this and you are thinking that somethings sound familiar in your relationship, if you are made to feel uncomfortable or put down then It is possible that you are also in an abusive relationship.

There is so much support out there, you don't have to suffer alone, but you do need to reach out to someone.

Abuse comes in many forms. Physical, mental, sexual and financial are to name some of them. Coercive control was only made illegal 4 years ago and so at the time of my abuse it wasn't illegal.

My mission is to raise awareness so that no one ever suffers or thinks its normal to stay in a relationship that breaks them down and makes them feel uncomfortable, worthless and like they have no where to go.

Rebuilding myself wasn't easy and it took time, but I did it and now I'm ready to teach other victims how to do the same.

By repeating 7 steps over and over again I was able to take myself from broken and lost to where I am now.

Let me share with you the 7 steps:

Step No 1 is gratitude. Every single morning as soon as you open your eyes, take out a book from your bed side drawer and write down 3-5 things you are grateful for, for that day. For me, some days it was the coffee in my hand, others it was my 2 boys or the food I had in my cupboards on the days I really struggled to find gratitude I gave thanks for my life, as I know it could have easily been taken away from me.

Step no 2 ..... Practice affirmations, write down 3, and repeat them to yourself all day, sometimes in your head, sometimes out loud, you could even stand in front of a mirror and say them to yourself. I CAN, I AM, I WILL , followed by anything you want, this tells the brain that what we are saying has already happened and therefore helps us achieve it

Step no 3.... Find 3 things that you are proud of yourself for, for that day, 3 things you forgive yourself for and 3 things that you commit too that day, these , for me, were hard, and I really struggled with them, sometimes they even reduced me to tears as i found it hard to tell myself I was proud or that I forgive.

Step no 4.... Move, move your body, have a dance, go for a walk go for a run, join a gym or jump up and down in your kitchen whilst listening to your favourite song. By moving we release chemicals in the brain that make us happy.

Step 5... Your Diet is so important if you put rubbish into your body you will feel like rubbish, fill your body with wholesome fresh food, vitamins and minerals and always ensure that you drink lots of water, 3ltrs a day is a minimum for me, if you can't drink water, try flavoured water, build it up over time.

Step 6 .... Practice relaxation, this could be anything from reading to meditation, to sitting in a quiet room having a cuppa. Watching television is not relaxing.

Step 7 .... Self-Love, every single day practice self-love, whether it be looking in the mirror and telling you that you love you! Buying yourself some flowers or getting your nails done. There are many things you can do to practice self-love.

In my 121 and online coaching I tell my clients that if they can't love themselves then how can they expect anyone else to love them. If they don't respect themselves how can they expect anyone else to respect them, and if they can't be thankful for what they have right now, no matter how small then how can they receive more.

I have dedicated my life to helping women move from being a victim to becoming a survivor and I would love to be able to help you.

Thank You for reading my story

Gemma x

ABOUT THE AUTHOR

GEMMA EVANS

www.gemmaevans.org

Hey, I'm Gemma a Self-love and Confidence Coach & Health and Wellness Mentor.

My passion in life is to teach females worldwide that self-love is the most important love of all.

After my dad committed suicide, suffering from a nervous breakdown myself and breaking free from a domestically abusive relationship, rebuilding myself mentally, physically and emotionally was my only option.

Now I teach women how to do the same and take back their power.

Sharing my story is so important to help other women realise that they can take their power back after abuse of any kind and it all starts with self-love.

My Warrior Women Academy is a safe environment for Women globally and my Women Who Can Mentorship programme will teach you how to take back your confidence and improve your health & wellness.

Connect with me

https://www.facebook.com/
groups/WarriorWomenAcademy/

Www.gemmaevans.org

I dedicate this chapter to Women World Wide fighting for a better life 🤍

#IfICanYouCanToo

 facebook.com/gemmaevans.org

HELEN ELIZABETH

*B*ut Still, I Rise

My name is Helen Elizabeth, I am 37 years old and live in Cheshire with my two beautiful daughters, 7 years and 11 months, my partner and our family dog George.

I write this chapter a different person to the woman I begin to talk about and I don't believe anyone could go through life and be subjected to the life experiences I have had and still be the same person, some would debate a sane person, but I live to tell of my experiences, somewhat tarnished but with a strength and character of a once broken woman who used the light of her daughter to bring her back from the brink.

Sometimes I wonder, did this life really happen to me, how can one girl grow up with an abusive mother, almost raped aged 11 years and sexually assaulted at 18 years by two complete strangers, join the police force and become the victim of systematic abuse and have an abusive marriage. Then I see the physical scars and the memories are so clear I have no doubt it did.

I often wondered about the kind of woman I would be had my life been different, but I try not to dwell. I can't change the past, but I do have some control over the present and the future, and I intend to live in the moment of each and every day that I continue to be blessed with. This is by no means an easy feat, as life continues, we will inevitably encounter obstacles and troubles, but it's our mindset that allows us to overcome these and move forward to live our life the way we choose, though we may have to accept that life is never going to fulfil all of our dreams and expectations.

I have had more than my fair share of hard times and countless battles, not only with others but with myself too and those I feel are the hardest to overcome. I may not have known the reason why at the time, yet every crisis is an opportunity to close one door and open more doors of opportunities and create new adventures and possibilities which we may not immediately be aware of or even expected.

I now know why I have had my hard times and struggles and if it wasn't for them, I wouldn't be here to share my experiences with you today, I share them in the hope that I can inspire you, motivate you and maybe even comfort you, so you know you are not alone. I always endeavour to be honest and I will tell you now, there were times when I would sit and wonder why me?

What have I done to deserve this? Especially in my younger years, when I saw no way out, no light flickering at the end of the tunnel, I wanted to give up, but I didn't, I kept fighting. Some battles took more out of me than others but each and every one of them made me the woman I am today, and I write this proud to be her.

I grew up on a council estate in Salford with my dad, mother, three sisters and a younger brother and a constant abundance of animals. My mother was incredibly abusive, I bare many a scar that remind me of the trauma she caused both me and my siblings.

With a father whom I idolised working all the hours he could to provide, we were left in the care of our mother when not at school. You would think being in the care of a parent was the safest place a child could be, but this wasn't the case. In fact my first memory is of my youngest sister Amy having her nappy changed by our mother, dad was working otherwise he would have been the one changing the nappy as mum wasn't a very maternal person, mum was kneeling on the floor in front of the fireplace, Amy was lay on her back and wriggling about like a little worm, I remember Amy giggling away, such a happy sound and I went over to them, I loved my sisters and enjoyed helping in any way I could.

I asked my mum if I could help, she told me to fill a jug with water and bring it to her, so I excitedly went in to the kitchen, filled a jug with cold water and happily danced my way back into the living room, I sat on the floor next to my mum and sister, placed the jug of water to the left of my mum, I sat eagerly awaiting my next instruction to help, as mum wet a cloth with the water I had just enthusiastically brought, I started to play with my little sister and without any warning my head jolted backwards, my mum had hold of my hair and pulled my head backwards, mum was shouting at me because the water was cold, I can't remember saying anything back I just started to cry at the pain and mum let go of me, my little sister then started to cry too.

Mum then started to put my sisters nappy on, it was the old style terry towelling nappies, where you have to use the safety pins to secure them, my mum wasn't gentle with Amy who then cried louder because mum had accidentally stuck her in the stomach with the safety pin, well at least I think it was an accident.

I could see the crimson red speckles of blood slowly become absorbed by the white terry towelling nappy, I told my mum I could see the blood and that she had just hurt Amy with the safety pin, within a split second my mum had taken the same safety pin she was trying to secure Amy's nappy with and stuck it in my arm, I immediately started to recoil and cry telling my mother to stop, I don't recall how many times my mum stuck the pin in my arm I just remember crying hysterically. Mum finished Amy's nappy, got up and walked away, leaving Amy and I crying on the floor. I lay next to Amy trying to console her, I was five years old and Amy just a few months.

This was the first of many painful memories I have of the woman I called mum.

This was the kind of abuse we were subjected to over the years, my mum would beat us and leave us to go without food, stick darts in our hands, place an iron on our hands, on one occasion she tried to get me to give my brother detergent in his sippy cup, so when my dad fell poorly after she made him a drink it didn't take me long to believe she had tried to poison him in some way.

On one Friday night she decided to leave my dad with the five children, she stood up told my dad she didn't love him nor us children and left. I needed answers and the following day I went to find her at my aunties house, she didn't want to see me, she dragged me out of the house, beat me and left me in the middle of the road and walked away from me. Although initially heartbroken when she left, we felt a huge relief when we realised she wasn't coming back, and we would no longer be subjected to her abusive behaviour.

Unfortunately that wasn't the only abuse I have been subjected to over the years, at the tender age of 11 years old, in the summer of 1993, I was on my way home from a summer fair with my friend riding our bikes, when we were riding across a railway bridge, I noticed a male walking towards us on the left side of the bridge, as I started getting closer to the male I began to speed up as I wanted to pass him as quickly as possible, something about him made me feel uncomfortable.

He was still on the left side of the bridge and I was on the right, as I approached him, he took one of his hands out of his jeans and lunged towards me knocking me to the floor, I was entangled in my bike, the male whilst holding me down managed to move my bike as best as he could, with his torso he was pressing me into the ground, I could barely breathe due to the pressure on my chest.

I was trying with all my might to scream, but I could barely get a word out, only small helpless sounds came out, he had one hand down his open jeans and was masturbating and with his other hand he was trying to pull my cycling shorts down, he eased the pressure on my chest, I was screaming at him to stop, telling him No, I was screaming for my friend, screaming for anyone to come anyone to help me.

I was hitting him and trying to push him off me with one hand and trying to stop him from puling my cycling shorts down with the other, he was licking my face, trying to put his tongue in my mouth, his breath was terrible, I had never smelt anything like it, his teeth were dirty, I was violently moving my head from side to side to prevent him from putting his tongue in my mouth. He was groaning, I was hysterical, fighting for what felt like my life and then out of nowhere there was a loud noise and it startled him, he got to his knees and ejaculated over me, got to his feet and ran off towards the steps I had just climbed minutes earlier and he was gone, leaving me broken on the floor.

I jumped up, arranged my clothing, grabbed hold of my bike and cycled as fast as my eleven year old legs could take me, I was clearly in a state because two police officers saw me and jumped out of their van to help me when I broke down. They never caught the male and I often wondered if they still have the DNA sample on file.

I was once again subjected to a sexual assault when I was 18 years, I was on a train sat by myself for a short while, I was sat next to the window, the train was relatively empty when an older male came and sat next to me. I didn't think anything of it and was keeping myself to myself, when suddenly I felt a hand on my left leg, I froze. I held my breath for a few seconds trying to take in what was happening, a million thoughts were racing through my head.

The man had placed his bag on his lap, whether this was to hide his erection or to cover up what he was doing I don't know, however he continued caressing my leg with his right hand, moving higher and higher until he reached my groin area. I grabbed his hand turned to him and told him to get the fuck off me followed by a barrage of expletives as you can imagine. I then burst out crying, I couldn't believe this could happen to me again, what was so wrong with me?

Passengers alerted the conductor and the police were called, luckily we had alerted the conductor before we stopped at the next station, Birmingham New Street, they were therefore able to keep everyone on the train. I spoke with police; gave them a detailed description and they searched the train for the male.

As I was still in my seat, they brought the same male back to me for identification purposes, I confirmed it was the same man however he had tried to disguise himself and changed not only his clothing but also his facial accessories and hair too. Clearly he knew what he was doing. We went to court, his lawyer was just as bad as the him, trying to make out I was lying, and the offender would have never done such a thing, it turned out it wasn't the first time this pervert had been arrested for sexual offences, he was found guilty and sentenced to time in prison.

When you think over 90% of sexual assaults are committed by a perpetrator the victim knows, you can see how unlucky I was to be sexually assaulted on two separate occasions by complete strangers.

All of my experiences and positive interactions with the police officers I had encountered, helped me with my decision to join the police force, So in 2003, following a lengthy process I joined one of the largest police forces in the UK. I knew I would be a good police officer; my experiences would enable me to have empathy and understanding and be able to assist victims of crime in a way a lot of other officers may not be able to.

However, within weeks I saw the negative side within the force, where police officers despicable behaviours towards members of the public were both, racist, abuse of power and sometimes criminal, from an officer dropping his trousers in front of me, rubbing his erect penis on a night out whilst asking me if it made me moist, telling me I wanted it and asking if my pussy was wet, when I started challenging such behaviours, it led me on a path of bully-ing, harassment and sex discrimination for requesting a flexible working pattern once I'd had my daughter, being told by my Chief Inspector "Helen, you are a woman who has just had a baby and trying to return to work full-time in a 24-hour emergency service.

Unfortunately you cannot have it all, you were aware of this before you had a baby", which resulted in me seeking legal advice and taking the police force down the route of a lengthy employment tribunal process, culminating in settling out of court and getting ill health retirement from the police force. This was because I was suffering from severe depression, caused and exacerbated by the treatment from the police force along with my abusive husband, sever hemiplegic migraines and hemicrania continua (HC) headache disorder following a head trauma after being assaulted at work.

Then their was my marriage, well the less said about that the better, from my mother in law telling me if she had a knife she would have stabbed me, then telling me on my wedding day she didn't like me and never wanted me to marry her son, to her son being physically abusive on a couple of occasions and regularly emotionally abusive, calling me fat, disgusting and an embarrassment.

Saying the diagnoses of severe depression confirmed what he already knew, that I was a psycho, telling me he never wanted our daughter, he only married me because other people wanted me and forcing me to make a choice between our marriage and a pregnancy, to attacking me and pinning me on the sofa to go through my mobile phone on Christmas day in the presence of our distraught daughter. At one point I was a woman on the brink of giving up and ending my own life and only stopped when I saw my daughters beautiful face pop up on my mobile phone.

So why do I share this with you, It would be easy to live my life blaming others for their mistreatment of me and ending up in a vicious cycle of victim mentality and self-sabotage, however, holding on to anger is like drinking poison and waiting for the other person to die. From a young age, I realised you have to forgive those who caused you harm, upset and hurt. That forgiveness does not mean you are weak, the forgiveness is not for the other person, it's for yourself, no matter what happened to you, life is a gift and so incredibly worthwhile.

Terrible things do and will happen, but that doesn't mean we allow those things to define who we are. They may shape and mold us, but they don't have to define us, because each and everyone of us deserves to be happy, and what actually defines us, is how we react to the circumstances and any subsequent decisions we make following on from that, we are who we choose to be, not what we have been subjected to and survived, so don't be a prisoner to your circumstance, reclaim your power and use your voice and story as a weapon. We have no control on how our story begins, but we do have control on how our story ends.

By the end of this chapter you will see I am a living example of that.

Though I have had my tough times, I live a fulfilling and happy life.

I have been blessed with two amazing daughters and I have a wonderful partner who supports me with my health, ambitions and dreams.

I had the honour of playing volleyball for England and travelled to many beautiful countries creating a lasting love for travel.

Since I divorced and retired from the police force, I have gone from strength to strength, along with graduating from university with a bachelor's degree in abuse studies, I have gained diplomas in life coaching and Cognitive behavioural therapy (CBT), I have become a bestselling author, international motivational speaker, an international speaker on communication skills and influencing people, I have started a business and created courses on effective communication and how to influence people, and this is only the beginning for me.

I am due to release my second book "The Truth Behind The Uniform" an expose of my time within the police force and what I witnessed police subject people to.

Despite the negative aspects of being in the police force I found I had a great passion for communicating with people, I enjoyed listening to them and helping them in the most difficult time of their lives, I learnt how powerful communication can be and through rigorous training, how we can influence people with the art of communication and how adapting communication techniques can have the desired result, whether that be money, promotion, new clients or when I was in the police, saving and protecting lives and gathering information to solve crimes.

Having taught people the skills I acquired over the years and enjoying it immensely when seeing those skills put into action and obtaining their desired result, I decided I wanted to help more people learn the importance of communication in order to help them advance their business, careers and relationships. So I started an online course for people to learn these skills at a pace that suits them, as well as offering this service to private businesses and corporate companies.

Within this chapter I would like to share with you some basic advice on how you too can develop your communication and influencing skills.

Whether you're an entrepreneur, small business owner or an employee wanting to further develop your career, it is inevitable that you acquire exceptional and effective communication skills for your success, and the success of your business and career. No matter what you do, developing effective communication skills can help you reach your full potential. Communicating effectively is needed in business, work place and in personal life.

For example, to have the ability to speak appropriately with a wide variety of people whilst maintaining good eye contact, to demonstrate a varied vocabulary and adapt your communication style and language to suit your audience, to appropriately present your opinions and ideas, actively listen effectively, write clearly and concisely, and work well in a group, all require good communication skills. Many of these are essential skills that employers seek and are required if you want to develop and be successful in business.

I would like to share a situation where I personally had to adapt my communication technique to achieve the desired result.

I had one incident where we attended a house as a concern for welfare called in by the ambulance service, the person in question was suffering with mental health issues and was trying to end their life by cutting themselves with pieces of glass, as we approached to try prevent her from doing further harm to herself she would try to attack us with the glass and as per our training we would shout for her to get back. The first thing the guys wanted to do was use their CS spray and physically take her to the ground to disarm her, but it was clear from what she was saying she was struggling with something and didn't think we would understand.

I asked them to give me a minute with her and let me talk to her, I asked her what she thought we wouldn't understand. I asked her to talk to me and I would listen and how did she know we didn't understand if she didn't give me the opportunity to listen. I think it was one of the first times she had ever been treated with respect by the police and asked how we could help instead of physically man handling her, and not use force to restrain her, the first time someone was willing to listen. Slowly she began to calm down and share her story with me, I listened to her empty her soul. She was so broken and traumatised, she didn't think someone like me would understand her pain.

When she finished, she was calmer and more at ease with me. I wanted her to know she was not alone, so I took it upon myself to take the glass from her, hold her hand and sit with her on the sofa, I shared with her a demon of my own, my own story of sexual assault when I too was a child. She broke down crying and gave me a hug followed by "you do understand". I managed to gain her trust, get her to go to the hospital in the ambulance and attend with her, I wanted her to know she wasn't alone, people do care and understand that she can get help required and that she is worth living.

Sometimes all somebody wants is someone to listen, because when you actively listen to someone, you will always find a way to connect with them and in turn find a way to get the desired result. This can be a result in many forms including money, career development, sales, relationships and even lifesaving situations.

So how do we communicate, why is it so important and how can we use communication to influence people and achieve the desired results we want.

Communication is the simple act of transferring or the

exchanging of information from one location to another. This can be done by using your voice (vocally), in a written form- this could be hand written letters or notes, using printed or digital media such as books, websites, social media, magazines or e-mails, visually, by using graphs, charts, maps and drawings, or non-verbal communication- this is using body language, gestures and the tone and pitch of voice.

Your communication skills are measured on how well you can transmit and receive the information. Some maybe better at communicating vocally rather than in writing and vice versa.

However, being able to communicate effectively is considered the most important of all life skills.

So, what is the importance of communication skills?

Communication skills are particularly important for:

- Forming contacts, developing and maintaining relationships
- • Giving and collating information
- • Understanding the needs of others and expressing personal needs
- • Giving and receiving guidance and support
- • Decision making and problem solving
- • Influencing other people's behaviours and attitudes

- • Making an impact
- • Anticipating and predicting others behaviour
- • Taking control and regulating power

There are various skills involved in effective communication and these can be practiced enabling you to become a more effective communicator. Many of these skills work together therefore making it important to practice where possible.

Verbal communication and active listening are two of the most important of these skills.

Effective questioning is an essential skill in verbal communication, asking the right questions can gather the correct information quickly and effectively also allowing you to build a rapport and later influence

Questioning can be used to:

- Start a conversation
- • Obtain important information
- • Build rapport
- • Include someone in a conversation
- • Show interest in a person

Open and closed questions are the two main types of questions to be used, these were the most effective questions we used in the police force when interviewing suspects and victims alike.

Open Questions

An open question is a question that cannot be answered with a simple "yes" or "no" response, the question is phrased to demand further discussion and an elaborative answer.

Examples include:

- "What did you do over the weekend?"
- "Where do you see yourself in five years?"
- "What would you like to gain from this course?"

Open questions are meant to gather more information and therefore will take longer to answer, but they encourage a more active involvement in the conversation. As a rule, in order to gather more information, the questions asked should start with one of the five W's and one H, these are considered to be the basic information gathering open questions.

Who?

What?

Where?

When?

Why?

How?

Closed Questions

Closed questions are intended to obtain a shorter response

often a "Yes" or "no" response or at least a one or two word answer.

Examples include:

- "Did you walk to work?"
- "Did you send that e-mail?"
- "Do you want to earn more money?"
- "Can I help you with that?"

Closed questions are often used so the person who is asking the questions remains in control of the conversation.

Closed questions do not encourage conversations; however, skilled communicators have the ability to keep the conversation alive by elaborating further.

A closed question need not be limited to a one-word answer.

In the first example above, the other person might simply respond yes or no. However, if they wanted to continue the conversation they may elaborate further and say:

- "No, I drove today, I have a tennis lesson after work and don't want to be late. How about you?"
- "No, I drove today, but isn't the parking a nightmare? Tomorrow I'm going to use the train. What about you?"
- " Yes, I did, it's a lovely day and I wanted to get some exercise and fresh air. Did you drive? Was the traffic bad?"

Closed questions are fantastic for time restricted discussions and can be used to focus specifically on a subject and to obtain clear and concise answers.

They are also a great way to establish areas of common interest when wanting to build a rapport.

I would like to give you a small questioning exercise to make you more aware of the types of questions you use in your next conversation.

During your next conversation and when you feel comfortable, this could be a personal situation or professional try asking them at least one open and one closed question and see if you notice a difference in the response you receive.

Try and notice:

- The length of the answer
- The information given
- The tone of the respondents' voice
- The respondents body language

Influencing people

How can we influence someone?

When people think of influencing a person they often think about manipulation, however there is a distinct difference between the two.

Manipulation does not work long term, there is no rapport or trust between the manipulator and the person being manipulated as inevitably the deception and lies will be discovered. It only works in the short term due to lack of information and experience on the behalf of the person being manipulated and once the person sits back and evaluates the situation more critically, they we be able to see the red flags and warning signs were there all along.

However, influencing people is a process that you need to undertake and if done correctly it works long term. You have to build a rapport and establish trust. It's a process that is practical and actionable and one that is measurable, predictable and repeatable. When followed correctly, it can be used by anyone in any situation.

"Influence is persuasion, persuasion is helping people come to their own most logical conclusion which just happens to be one that we share, persuasion is about being a more effective communicator and getting the best outcome for everyone involved " ~ David Lakhani

When people think about influencing, they naturally worry, are we wearing the right outfit, will I say the right thing, will I manage to communicate to the audience in the right way. However, I truly believe that observation is the foundation of influencing people effectively. The majority of your work in influencing people is actively listening and observing, it may surprise you but saying nothing at all is how you will learn to influence.

When you focus on your audience, observe how they try to influence you, because what they are doing, is showing you how they want to be influenced and that's how you will connect and in turn influence.

Your ability to influence effectively is an everyday skill that can benefit you greatly. As stated earlier, influencing is not about manipulating people, it's about understanding how other people think and see things. If you can understand what is going on in the mind of another person and understand the way they think, it will enable you to see things from their point of view more effectively. When trying to influence you need to remember, the way you can be influenced does not guarantee your desired outcome. As you would be trying to use "Your method of influence" rather than "Their method"

Being able to see things from the other persons perspective is beneficial when understanding which influencing strategy to use. Flexibility in your communication style is key.

In order to successfully influence, you need to establish a relationship, build rapport, gain trust and make a connection with them, you need to adapt your communication style and identify the audience's personal and emotive triggers in order to obtain the best and required results from the audience you are trying to influence.

Influencing requires empathy, a subtle and indirect approach is more effective than a more direct and forceful approach.

I want to share with you how I teach my clients to have the

mind set of an influencer. This set you in good stead for becoming better at influencing yourself.

There are three main points

The Focus,

The Goal,

The Purpose,

THE FOCUS

As a communicator your focus should be on one thing and that is your audience, it's always about them, never you. Most people find that one simple piece of advice a game changer.

If you are a teacher, it's about your students' needs,

If you are a salesperson, it's about what your customers wants,

If you are a speaker it's about your audience,

It's always about them, it has to be about them because they are the one you are trying to influence, and when you make it about them, we start to ask the right questions instead worrying about everything to do with ourselves.

We then start to ask ourselves,

What do they need to hear?

What will they gain from this?

What do they want from me?

What value can I share that's going to really impact them?

From the moment you realise it's not about you, you will feel differently, your energy changes and it allows us to focus on being rather than being caught up in our own mind.

We tend to focus on perfection, making sure we hit every point we set out to say, making sure the delivery was impactful, but rarely does anyone give a perfect speech. Therefore, we have the wrong goal.

Goal

If your focus is on the audience, then you goal is to connect with the audience. Therefore, your goal needs to change from perfection to connection.

Perfection is about us, connection is about them, so your goal should be connecting with the audience, because when you make it about them and when you connect with that audience all the imperfect deliveries don't matter.

People will not listen or be influenced by you if you do not connect or resonate with them, if you want to move people and influence them we need that connection, therefore our focus is on the audience which means our goal is not one of perfection, its now connection, so the connection becomes your purpose.

Purpose

When we give speeches you need to ask yourself, what is my purpose here? Your purpose is to engage with them, but what do I mean to engage? To engage means to grab hold of their attention, to captivate them, in today's society we seem to do a lot of talking at people when we should be talking with people, we need to move away from text messaging and electronic communicating and move back to having conversations, a conversation is a dialogue between two or more people, there's a back and forth and participation from all parties. Whether you are in a group or one on one there should be conversation, communication of back and forth, make it interactive by asking questions only then can we influence.

If you can remember that your focus is on the audience, your goal is not perfection it's connection with that audience, and your purpose is to engage that audience then you can start to communicate in a more influential manner. Because without engagement there's never any influence.

A combination of interpersonal and communication skills will help you to get the desired results. Here are a few simple tips to help get you started on developing your influencing skills.

1. BUILD A RAPPORT

You need to build a rapport with the person you are trying to influence, this is essential to your success. Building a rapport is the first step in gaining the trust of the person you are trying to influence. You need to make that person feel like they can trust you. It sounds like common sense but if a person likes and trusts you, there is a greater possibility that you will be able to influence them.

2. Actively LISTEN

Listening is the most powerful way to create that rapport and build that trust. You need to actively listen and demonstrate you are listening because listening creates understanding, and when you understand what your audience wants, you can influence. If someone feels valued they are more likely to be influenced by your point of view and the best way to listen is to clear your mind and focus on what is actually being said.

3. ASK QUESTIONS

We can all ask questions, but you need to ask the right kind of questions. As I demonstrated earlier ask open questions that draw people in, allow them to tell you more. Use the questioning techniques earlier in the chapter to lead people towards the answers you want. Sometimes it's as simple as rephrasing the question.

Try to avoid starting questions with "Why", this one word at the start of a question can automatically put them on the defensive. It's also accusatory. I learnt this many times within the police force, therefore, try starting the question with "What is it" I use this technique with my daughter all the time. It's as simple as changing "Why do you want to watch this movie again?" to "What is it about this movie that you like and enjoy so much?"

Chances are you have just laid the foundations to a conversation.

4. Mirroring body language

Mirroring the other person's physical and verbal behaviours to create a better rapport. Sounds a little creepy, however when done subtly it can have huge effect. Mirroring automatically tends to happen when two people know each other well, however mirroring can serve as a powerful influencing tool as it can lead your prospect to subconsciously believe that you are acting like them because you are their friend and like them. One of the easiest and most subtle techniques is to replicate the persons speech volume and pace.

5. SELL THE BENEFITS

Sell the benefits of your argument to the other person and try to see your position from their perspective. When you argue, you oppose your position against the position of the other person. Therefore, if you want to influence that person and build that rapport, you need to step out of your own world, and gently enter their world. Therefore, you need to become a student of your prospect.

6. BE RELAXED

A relaxed and natural demeanour is more likely to achieve a successful outcome rather than an emotional or demanding approach. Demonstrating a natural confidence will help to persuade others that your ideas are good.

7. INVEST YOUR TIME

Influencing isn't a quick fix. It can take time to develop empathy and awareness but you are more likely to get what you want if you play a long game.

The art of influencing doesn't come naturally to everyone. If you would like to improve your communication and develop your influencing skills.

Contact Helen for some invaluable courses to get you on your way to better communication skills and improve your ability to influencing people.

Helen is also available for speaking engagements

To book Helen contact hellohelenelizabeth@outlook.com

ABOUT THE AUTHOR

HELEN ELIZABETH

Lifestyle Coach, Communication and influencing coach, Motivational speaker, Best-selling author in The Woman I'm Becoming, Featured journalist on divorcedmoms.com and has been publish by the Huffington post.

Author of "The Truth Behind The Uniform", exposing racism and discrimination within the police force, to be released in May 2019

Helen is 37 years old and mother to her two girls ages seven years and eleven months. She currently resides in Cheshire with her partner, children and family dog George. After 14 years as a police officer Helen recently retired. Since retiring, Helen has completed a BA Hons in abuse Studies at Manchester University and also has a Diploma in Cognitive Behavioural Therapy and a Diploma in Life Coaching. As a youth Helen played volleyball, representing England on the international scene until joining the police at 21.

Helen is passionate about her daughters, determined to provide them the family life and love which she sadly missed out on in her childhood. She is committed to social justice, after experiencing sexism and discrimination during her career as a police officer, leading her to an employment tribunal case, as well as witnessing some of the injustices and tragedies to befall the less fortunate in society. She is an avid writer and hopes to further develop her career as an author and motivational speaker.

In sharing her message Helen hopes that she can provide inspiration and positive guidance to help people realise their true potential.

I am dedicating this chapter to my two incredible girls, Mia and Ava, without you both in my life I would not have the strength to strive to be the best I can be, I do so to inspire you both and be the loving mother every child deserves. You have shown me the true meaning of unconditional love and I am blessed each and everyday to be your mummy. I love you more than you will ever know.

I also dedicate this to my partner Paul for always believing in me and loving me without conditions. I love you all.

8

HELEN LEACH

a moment of trauma completely changes the path of our lives.

Usually for the worse.

What if I was to tell you that it also works the other way around?

A moment of clarity, Insight, Peace.

Can bring those broken off pieces back together.

Making us whole once again.

The only problem is that it took 20 years for someone to point that out to me, and another 3 years of learning and self-work before I was in a place that I could undo the initial trauma and find my own self harmony. It's all to do with the stories we tell ourselves and being brave enough to face and unravel them so we can find the inner truths.

These stories are always initially written to protect ourselves.

Unfortunately, they can over stay their welcome and begin to add to the burden of pain and sorrow that they were created to protect us from. New stories are created upon the old and weigh us down in our hearts. It is so easy to become lost and people have forgotten that they can rewrite these stories so that we can lift ourselves up once again.

Here are the stories that I have unfolded.

And how I have managed to rewrite my life for the better.

A friend of mine has gently told me that I have lived a cosmic car crash of a life. My mother likes to say that I have had a "difficult life". Both are correct but I also have heard the stories from others to know that I have had it quite easy too. But this is not a competition. Rather, each of us have our own journeys from which we need to learn so that we can grow and evolve. As a dear friend once said to me "sometimes the most important lessons come from the hardest moments". Never a truer word from such a beautiful wise soul. But we must also remember that we can learn from the most beautiful moments too. We should hold on to these in our hearts just as much, if not more.

Having been raised in a very intelligent family, expectations for me were high. Unfortunately, when I was a child, dyslexia was an unheard of condition. Quite simply, I just didn't get it. Numbers and words just never stuck. Academia was too ridged. It didn't allow for nuances, creativity or instinctual flow. Add to that I was very short sighted and had trouble with my hearing, to say I was glad to leave school is an understatement. New beginnings in a new city. Finally having the space to explore my own self and passions, to fall in love and out again. It was a time I always look back upon fondly.

Unfortunately, a casual night out with friends turned in to a desperate fight for survival. We were at a local night club and ended up chatting to a couple of lads and a girlfriend who'd accompanied them. So, I stayed and had the drink offered to me by one of the lads and soon enough I decided it was time to go home. I was feeling tired and woozy and knew I had classes the following day. They offered me a lift in their taxi as they said they were heading my way and again I thought, I will be ok as there is another girl here. I hopped in to the taxi first, reeling off my address to the driver and as I sat down it hit me. The full realisation of the setup had slapped me in the face as only one of the lads got in to the taxi closing the door behind him. The other two of the group jumped into the taxi behind.

You know when you are watching a film and you are shouting at the person to not to go down that dark flicking corridor because it has the scary music and the serial murderer there? Well, try living in that moment. I could see everything unfold and yet was powerless to avoid it. I tried to get out of the taxi before it reached my home but taxis lock their doors while in motion and he assured me he was just dropping me off. I told him that I did not want him to come inside as he forced his way in to my home and in to my room. I can't remember the number of times I told him to stop but I felt so physically weak and my mind was going in to pure panic as it was detaching from the events happening to me. Grateful to not to have to bear witness to the assault upon my body I followed the detachment and my soul left the room.

The following morning, was surreal. I knew I had to go to the morning class as compulsory attendance requirements were high. I also knew I had to go to the doctors as I was determined that this incident would not leave me with a child born of such violence. I booked my appointment on route to class and sneaked out of the lab to go to my appointment. While at the doctors I discovered the full extent of victim shaming that I was to receive. As he wrote my prescription, he called me a silly girl filled with contempt and disgust.

One of my housemates dismissed the event telling me that these things just happen and to get over it. My ex-girlfriend tried to use the situation to win me back and when that didn't work tried to kill me through strangulation. The final straw was when I confessed the whole event to my tutor as I knew I was going to struggle with my end of year exams. He decided in his wisdom to not stand up for me at the examination board and I was requested to withdraw from the course. A polite way of saying that they were kicking me off for failing one exam.

Aged 19 I was still a kid. The support system that I reached out to failed me and I felt the full shame, disgust, pain and anger of what had been done to me. I fell apart with a rage that was frightening. Inside my mind there was this eternal scream ripping through me and I turned to the only thing available to quieten that scream. I began using, abusing and quickly became addicted to a variety of drugs in a bid to lessen the scream of anger and pain that I felt within. For that first year I completely cut off my family and drowned in my new world. You know those things that they say drug addicts do in order to get their next fix? Well, that's all true too.

My 20's were dark drug induced hazy years. I am grateful that I cannot remember the details as the memorable highlights are enough to bring a tear to anyone's eye. I now realise that I was living, or rather surviving, the only way I knew how with the limited tools and support available. I lost my appetite for life and was full steam ahead to self-destruction. I didn't just press the self-destruct button; I was smashing it with my fist in defiant rage. I had lost so much weight that I stopped weighing myself when I dropped below 6 and half stone.

To forgive myself for those years has been the biggest and hardest lesson I have had to learn. Surprisingly, I managed to scratch together a degree qualification in Environmental Risk Management and created the first ever LGBT+ Student's Union Society in the University when others had previously failed. To this day I have no idea how that happened. It amazes me what we can still achieve even in our darkest days.

In our darkest places.

Even the smallest light can be blinding.

Let it lead you.

Let it heal.

The beautiful thing of having lived in the underworld of our society is that I got to meet the most interesting people. I was surrounded by drug addicts, dealers and prostitutes who would often lie and steal from you given half a chance but would also stand up, help and protect you. It all depended upon the depth of their pain on that day. Strangely many felt safe enough with me to share their stories. No-one chooses that life and their stories could break your heart a thousand times over.

It's taken me two decades to learned two things from that time.

Firstly, every single person in this world is just doing what they believe to be the best thing at that time given their circumstances, resources, support and mindset. Once I realised this, I knew I could forgive anyone for anything as most people who cause pain are just reacting from a place of pain. Instead of anger and hate, forgiveness and peace found its place within me and I learned to forgive all those who had hurt me.

Secondly, I cannot and will not judge others. For I have probably done it, or had it done to me, and if not, then I have held those who have. To judge others is to judge myself and I have done enough of that already. From a place of compassion, forgiveness and acceptance I have now found that people naturally come to me for support in their darkest times. I find it interesting that people now refer to me as inspiring, grounded, centred and calming. I actually find it amusing as I was anything but during my 20's and 30's.

In my late 20's I received my first break. My local temping agency got in contact with a 6 month contract as a filing clerk with the Environment Agency. Within 3 months I had completed the project and the team decided to keep me on as an Administrator.

As a reward, my boss organised a shadow day with the local river ecology team. I still remember standing in the middle of the beautiful Welsh countryside on a glorious sunny day, knee deep in a gentle river. For the first time in years I felt peace envelop me. I knew in that moment that I had to get a job with this team and after 3 attempts with some sneaky negotiating I was hired. The learning curve was immense and I quickly realised that it required a clear head. Bit by bit I got myself clean and just after my 30th birthday I was free from that drug induced world and have never once looked back.

In a plot twist, a year after getting clean my heart began to fail me. I spent my 30's bouncing around the cardiology wards with an obscurely diagnosed ventricular tachycardia. Basically, my heart was having regular fits within my chest and was unable to pump enough blood around my body. I quickly discovered that I had become over sensitive to the medication as it was clear my body was being defiant that I had polluted it quite enough with toxins already. I couldn't even have a cup of coffee without being hospitalised. Two operations later with the cardiologist informing me that they were unable to get it all, I knew I was in for the ride again soon.

Now, bearing in mind that my parents are both intelligent traditional biologists, having my Mum offer me energy healing in the form of Reiki came as a bit of a surprise. My parents stumbled upon Reiki themselves as my father's reflexologist sneaked it in at the end the sessions leaving my Dad with this unexplained heat going up his feet and legs.

Naturally, as all good traditional scientists would, we ran experiments utilising my dodgy heart as the subject in a blind study. I was the one blindfolded. Would you believe I could feel the energy healing so intensely over my heart it became unbearable? I could easily tell when healing was taken away or brought over my heart. Intrigued, I decided to study Reiki myself as I knew modern medicine was not helping me heal and I was becoming determined not to fall ill for a third time.

My second break came when my partner unexpectedly ended our relationship. Left homeless with two dogs and little money, I was grateful that I could turn to my parents for sanctuary. One morning my Mum pointed to an article in the paper that was discussing the current storyline in a popular radio show about a couple in an abusive relationship. At the end was "10 ways to spot if you are in an abusive relationship".

As I read each item and mentally ticked them off, my world fell away from under me. How did I not realise this? How was I so blind? The insidious nature of the development of such a relationship makes it imperceptible to recognise when you are living within it day after day but glaringly obvious to those who hear the stories from outside.

I am grateful to my Mum for finding the only way that I could accept such a revelation. The last time I went back to my home to collect what little belongings I had, I remember looking in to my ex's eyes questioning if I had got it all wrong. Was I wrong about the abuse? My ex wanted us to date again, so could there still be a chance to patch it all up? She smiled back at me and promptly let rip an almighty fart. The moment of doubt was broken and I never returned.

Now this may not sound like a lucky break. By losing every-thing, my home, my career, most of my money and belong-ings, and my own identity, I'd had the slate wiped clean. Crumpled and broken I surrendered all pretence of control over my life. Clearly, I wasn't getting this life thing right so it was time to let the Universe show me where I should be going. I was determined that I no longer wanted to be this victim again. I no longer wanted to carry this heavy weight of shame and pain so that others could target me rather than face their own pains.

Let the tears flow.

For the healing waters will cleanse your pains away.

I must warn you that tears are my physical response to most things in life. When I'm sad, I cry. When I'm overjoyed, I cry. Shock means tears. Relief, blub. Panic and anxiety, yep you've guessed it, water works. It's so easy to make me laugh-cry it hurts. It's like my personal emotional pressure value to life. Too much emotion? Let's release it via water-falls from the eyes. It works for me and I accept it even though everyone thinks I'm a little bit odd when they see me crying at a beautiful television advert.

Even in the depths of pain, I have found that it is hard to cry when my cute gremlin dog Minnie presses up to my face desperate to get her salt fix from the tears from my eyes. Whiskers tickling and her eyes glistening as she knows it always makes me laugh. Then she just sits upon my lap gazing up at me until I am fully calm again. What amazing healers these dogs can be! If it wasn't for my two beautiful dogs by my side making me feel protected and safe, I know my healing journey would not had been so successful. I had to heal so that I could be at my best for them.

So, I began looking in earnest to a new career. I love animals. I love my dogs. It made sense to learn how to help dogs and so I signed up for a Diploma in Canine Sports Massage and was inexplicably drawn to apply for the Diploma in Animal Healing with Elizabeth Whiter.

Now, I had never heard nor met this lady before and so I was requested to attend one of the healing evenings with an interview beforehand. As we sat there discussing my plans for the future and the fact that I had been accepted on to the canine massage course, Elizabeth Whiter jumped out of her seat, punched the sky with her fist whilst exclaiming a joyous "YES!!" But that really sums up our lovely Liz. An individual with so much passion and energy for her work she inspires and exhausts you at the same time just by watching her. I am amazed that somehow Liz saw into the core of me within that first meeting and glimpsed my potential. A potential that even I was unaware of. I am eternally grateful for the opportunity that Liz gave me by offering the last position on her Diploma that year.

And so, began my tuition in the world of animal healing and the biggest lesson Liz has taught me, anyone can train to be a good healer but in order to be a great healer you must first heal yourself. To clear the channel so that the healing energy is free to flow as unhindered as possible. When I started this course, I thought I was being taught how to help animals heal but I walked away with a deeper understanding of our own self-healing as well. The fact that each and everyone of us are connected and filled with such immense power. A network of light that brings us all together helping to raise us out of our disconnected and perceived sense of powerlessness.

Liz also taught me the importance of staying centred and protected. To be the calm in the storm and not allow the debris get caught up within ourselves. As Liz would say "making sure we are suited and booted before we face the day." Every morning I take myself through a simple yet effective mini meditation. A meditation that involves gratitude, grounding, centring, checking in with the chakras, conducting brain-heart breathing and connection, and setting up my protection.

It's amazing how much one can cover in a quick 10-minute meditation that makes all the difference for the day ahead. I can always tell when I have forgotten my morning meditation as I become all flighty, erratic and disjointed. The flow just doesn't happen.

Look deep within my dear.

For there you will see your true demons and angels.

And see that they are neither.

They are just the light and shadows of your soul.

Waiting for your embrace of acceptance.

True self-healing also comes from facing the shadows within. It is one thing to reach for the light in the Universe. To be always searching for the best in everyone and ourselves. But we can not do this at the cost of ignoring our own shadow selves. The areas we don't want to look upon. The pain, sadness, anger, addictions, the messy areas that we don't admit to ourselves, let alone allow anyone else to see.

I stumbled upon an advert for a workshop with a Shaman and Spiritual Mentor called Charlotte Gush. The day was focused on helping people to retrieve their power. Having known the extent of feeling powerless, this sounded good to me. As Charlotte would say "true healing is when those cracks become filled with gold." It was a powerful day focused on retrieving my personal power from a past life and from another individual.

Following that day, I knew I had to work with Charlotte further. I just loved her down to earth, no nonsense approach. Bringing nature back in to our lives. Listening to what nature has to tell us, the rhythms, ebbs and flows. How we are intimately linked to all around us and how we can work in harmony together. Learning to trust myself and my intuition once again.

Charlotte echoed Liz's wounded healer warning - a person who is wounded and finds purpose in healing others. To ensure that our healing does not become contaminated, we need to first heal ourselves. To become a clear channel for the work and from this place, people and things will come to us more easily.

I learned from Charlotte the tools and practices that I now use in my daily life to keep me on an even keel. The power of stone medicine to help when emotions become over-whelming. Breath work to shift stagnant energies within. The wisdom from observing that everything is cyclic, even our own healing. Learning from my ancestors and even helping them with their own healing journeys. Journeying within, below, and beyond all that we understand and know so that we can learn and expand.

Meeting and talking with the various aspects of myself, the child, the old lady, the critical self, the scientist, the believer and so many more. By objectively reflecting within, our stories are revealed and we are able to rewrite their meaning, power and direction. Bringing them together like abstract pieces of a kaleidoscope making a colourful whole picture of the soul.

I have always had a love for rescue dogs.

Their plight of pain, abandonment and loss.

Had always reflected what was in my heart.

As I have rescued them.

They have also rescued me.

The healing Animals Organisation, created by Liz, regularly organises trips abroad to help animals all over the world. I saw it as a great opportunity to put all my holistic animal therapies and techniques in to action in a baptism of fire kind of way. I also knew that this will probably be the only opportunity for me to experience this adventure as my heart condition was returning for a third round and experience telling me that another 3 to 4 years of my life would be difficult to say the least.

The rescue centre in Cyprus was what you'd expect, noisy, dusty, and over flowing with dogs of all shapes and sizes. We worked hard as a team to provide comfort, healing, nutritional and uplifting natural supplements, training and therapies of all kinds as required. The work was tiring yet rewarding as we witnessed incredible transformations of those in our care even within the short time we were there.

During my stay, I helped with the rescue's Freedom Flight. A weekly event whereby they transported adopted dogs to the airport and sent them on their way to their new forever homes in the UK. It truly amazes me how these volunteers work tirelessly to find better lives for those in their charge. As we sat outside the airport sipping decaffeinated coffee, one of the organisers noted that the plane was taking off and the dogs will soon be in their new lives.

Having worked personally with these individuals, my heart soared. It more than soared. It completed shattered open and the whole Universe of love just came pouring out like a cosmic jet stream. Breathe Helen, just breathe through it, I told myself. Throughout the rest of the trip, my heart kept on splitting open to allow this out pouring through. It almost knocked me off my feet many times in the days after.

Once I got home, I decided to focus on my health. I went on to the auto immune diet, gently built up exercise and within a month I was once again at the Cardiologist waiting for my test results. What do you know? They were all clear. No sign of my pesky arrhythmia at all! And I mean none. Even after both my surgeries there were residual aberrations remaining. The cardiologist was astounded and told me to carry on doing what I was doing. How could I tell him that the Universe poured through my heart and healed it? He's not going to find that cure in his text books.

It was also on this trip, after hearing the troubles that the other animal therapists were having with their business development, that I realised that I had to do something to help. MyPetsReview.com was born. I learned about websites, created and developed the first ever online review website for animal therapists and practitioners in the UK. I had found my purpose and calling in helping other healers and heart based businesses promote themselves online.

At the same time my beautiful husky Shida was blossoming. As a rescue dog herself she came with her own suffering but was finally in a place where she could fully express her own self. She became chatty with me and would playfully bop me on the arm with her paw if I was not paying attention. For two years she knew peace and happiness. Unfortunately, her liver began to fail her and her health took a drastic turn for the worst.

The biggest responsibility of being a healer is to recognise when the only compassionate course of action is to gently bring an end to the suffering. As much as I loved Shida and didn't want to let her go, I couldn't stand by and watch her suffering fits from her blood poisoning. Five times I have made this impossible decision, twice I have had to carry out the act by my own hand. As plans were made with the vet, I began seeing little white feathers everywhere. On that morning, Liz with her circle of students tuned in during their mediation to help Shida on her journey.

Liz even channelled that it should be a beach meditation without even knowing that was the place of her last morning walk. Shida sat on the sofa next to me, leant in to me and gently passed away in to my lap. For two weeks afterwards, I saw the little white feathers everywhere. I mean hundreds every single day. Now when ever I see a small white feather it reminds me of Shida and her blowing undercoat. Shida is the husky that can be seen on the home page of MyPetsReview.com as a memorial to the wonderful support that we can provide our furry friends and that they provide us.

Following Shida's passing, I knew I had become stagnant and needed to be nearer like-minded people. I moved to Sussex where Liz and some of my colleagues, who had become close friends, lived. A second trip to Cyprus involved a spirit whispering in to my ear as I glanced at a new inmate at the Cypriot Pound, "he will be perfect for Minnie". Sure enough, a few weeks later Minnie was greeting this new terrier cross, Freddie, with play bows and excited "uffs".

Within ten minutes the pair were running around the house having the time of their lives. Yes, he is perfect for Minnie. They sleep together, play together, and generally cause mischief together. Shida, being the aloof husky that she was, had a maternal watchfulness over Minnie but was never the companion that Minnie craved. Now she has a friend who curls up to her as they made their own version of yin and yang.

Ignorance is not bliss.

Ignorance is accepting what we do not want to know.

Ignorance is giving our blessings to continued destruction.

It is hard to ignore that we live in a rape culture. The shame that others place upon the victims in an attempt to justify the actions of the perpetrator. Using phrases such as "boys will be boys" serves nothing except alleviate their responsibility for their own actions. To justify themselves by blaming the woman's choice of clothes, or that by buying a drink enables the right to take her body. Good grief, the number of times I have been grabbed, pinched, and kissed without consent is ridiculous. This truth will be echoed by every woman within our society today.

We are taught from a young age that we have no rights over our own bodies. Family members insisting you have to hug and give a kiss to the creepy uncle or friend of the family whose hands are always straying. When I was young, I was often tickled until I cried by a family member even though I would tell him to stop. He said I enjoyed it. The programming was being subtly installed so that when I was attacked, I wouldn't make a fuss. I would keep quiet and doubt my own sense of right and my own self-worth.

What I have since realised that rape has very little do with sex. In fact, it is all about power and control. Men are raised in a society which places many tough and hard expectations upon them. To live a life of toxic masculinity that transforms easily and quickly in to the wounded masculine. They end up in pain, feeling powerless and looking for an easy way to regain that power and control. What better way than to take it from another person in an act that is gratifying in more than one way? In a way that is accepted, dismissed and ignored by our society.

What is rarely spoken about is the transference of energy during these violent encounters as the perpetrator quite literally transfers his pained energy in to his victim. The victim's body holds on to this energy and it easily becomes toxic if it is not cleansed out. The cells of the body also remember the violence.

I realised it was important for me to heal from my sexual assault, to cleanse the energy out and heal my body's cell memory. Womb breathing and forms of yoga help to relax and open up the pelvis. Jade egg practices to help cleanse, re-sensitise and heal. There are many sexual healing mentors who have stepped up to help with this intimate wound and I have found Layla Martin inspiring, fun and totally understanding of the broader aspects of sexuality and healing.

We also have the task of showing those men who are now growing up, our brothers, sons and nephews, that they can stand in their own power without the need to diminish another's. By standing together we can achieve so much more in this world. This world does not have to be one of struggle and competition but one of support, collaboration and celebration.

> "Courage is stepping over your invisible threshold and committing to who you are becoming even before you know who that is."
>
> Charlotte Gush – Shamanic Way

After, three years of healing, forgiving, grounding and learning to bring myself back to centre, I started to feel a presence by my side. I have always sensed spirits since I was a young kid. My family, being the good traditional scientists that they were brought up to be, dismissed my stories as an over active imagination. I quickly learned to ineffectively block off these presences and developed a strong fear of these unknown night time entities. Now wiser and having learned some skills in protection and connecting with spirit, I began to ask this new entity who they were. I just could not get an answer and could not work out who it was.

Then one day during a discussion with Charlotte, she informed me that over time pieces of our soul could detach. Could it be that when I detached myself from the trauma of my attack 23 years ago that I had in fact broken a huge piece of my soul away and it had never reattached back? I sensed in to this entity and felt only kindness, love and compassion.

I also sensed the truth of what I had for so long ignored. I knew that finally, after all my healing, my soul piece felt safe enough to come near and potentially return home to me. So, plans were laid to do a soul retrieval... and got delayed....procrastinated...avoided. I never knew how a soul retrieval would go. Tears, joy, definitely a lot of emotions. Remembrance. Did I really want to remember what I had disconnected from? I was afraid. I fell ill with acute exhaustion and even went to the Doctors for tests not realising how it was all related.

The day came. A day before a powerful New Moon and I felt as prepared and fuck-it-let's-do-it-anyway as I could be. Charlotte, being my mentor, guide and witness as we worked together bringing this soul piece home. At the end of the session the desolate emptiness was filled and I finally felt whole. My persistent heaviness lifted and I felt lighter, freer. I am more focused, creative, and that acute tiredness evaporated. I still feel this way to this day and I look back in gratitude.

This has indeed been a difficult path that I have travelled. I have looked in to the eyes of death too many times to count and yet I find myself mesmerised with wonder by the ceremonies and memorials to death and the dead.

I have immense compassion and patience for those who are lost or at the early stages of their own healing path. For I have lived and survived the underworld of our modern society and have known the stories and pains of those who reside there. I am able to forgive through compassion and understanding.

I have also learnt that I must hold my boundaries firmly with compassion and fairness. Just because I can forgive and understand does not mean that others can take advantage.

I am still learning.

I am learning to be true to myself.

And that as the healing continues.

I am the only one responsible for my own path.

I hold no regrets.

For I love who I am and this path was the only way to become me.

I love the work that I do and the people who I choose to be in my life.

I love my life.

I love.

> "Ones willingness to 'fit in' and be accepted often overwrites the souls purpose and causes those who bend to its will to wander through their days disconnected, even lost...
>
> We all have a choice, a choice to bend or a choice to attain a statuesque posture, look above the crowds and create something of meaning for ourselves"
>
> Charlotte Gush – Shamanic Way

ABOUT THE AUTHOR

HELEN LEACH

Helen Leach is a fully qualified and insured Holistic Dog Therapist and experienced Website Geek and there is nothing she loves more than bringing these two worlds together within her work.

To help support her colleagues in the animal care world, Helen has created the first ever online review website specifically for animal therapists and practitioners in the UK called MyPetsReview.com. With her love for rescue animals, this website also provides a platform for Animal Rescue Charities to be supported and promoted free of charge.

Helen has also created a Facebook support group called

"Holistic Pet Business - Support and guidance for animal professionals" where lead experts in business provide free advice and guidance to help animal practitioners grow their own businesses.

You will often find Helen at the numerous conferences and pet shows talking and promoting holistic animal therapies and techniques. These include Animal Energy World Conference, National Pet Show, Discover Dogs London, Crufts and many more.

Helen also runs a successful business helping animal and heart-based companies build and maintain their websites both within the UK and internationally. Her services are aimed at helping new small entrepreneurial businesses get online through to supporting International Schools, and she is quickly being recognised as being the go-to person within her industries. To find out more about her website creations and how you too can create a soulful website for your business, you can look at her website HelenLeach.co.uk and her Facebook page "Soulful Websites - Easy way to create beautiful heart based WordPress sites".

In her spare time, Helen spends her days at animal rescue centres across the world bringing her therapy skills to those that need it the most.

"By working together, we can all heal, we can all raise up higher, we can all reach for the stars!"

9

JO BOSWELL

a corporate career as an accountant at a huge mobile phone giant was how it all started, I earned a good salary, had lots of friends and lived my life to the highest standards - you could even go as far as saying I was a little high maintenance! (I beg to differ though!).

I was happy, I had a lovely boyfriend, I lived at home with my parents but we were looking for a place to live - my path was clear and I knew where I was going, I was full of ambition.

But then, things at work changed, a new boss, the person I worked with left and my boyfriend at the time, dealt with some things at work that changed him (he'd just joined the emergency services and as a young person saw things some people never see in a lifetime). My easy lifestyle, my amazing job and my perfect relationship all started to become hard work - all at the same time.

I was only 21 and I wanted freedom, I didn't want to deal with the reality of life and having to make a relationship work, I didn't want to work for someone who I didn't bond with and I certainly didn't want to work with the new boy in the office. But, I was young, I didn't think of the consequences of my actions and I made choices that in hindsight I shouldn't have.

I ended the relationship, I started drinking and going out more with people from work, I stopped putting effort into my work.

Before I knew what was happening I was caught in a spiral of a life I didn't enjoy, I was secretly sleeping with the 'new boy' in the office, smoking and drinking too much and trying to burn the candle at both ends.

Then one day, my life changed, forever.

We'd gone out on a secret date, a relationship that was nothing, we'd decided that there should be no strings attached, he wanted to see other people, I wasn't that bothered. We'd gone to watch a movie in a town about 15 miles from home so nobody would see.

But I cried and then laughed and then cried and then something struck me - could I be pregnant? No way, not possible!

We went back to his and bought a test, I did it and then went downstairs to have a cigarette, after all, I wasn't pregnant, but before I'd even got downstairs a voice shouted at me, don't light that....and I knew.

I was 22 and pregnant by someone I wasn't even in a relationship with, someone who I worked with, someone who I had to keep this whole thing a secret with, what would my parents think, I lived at home, I had an amazing car, but it was on finance - I was mortified.

I don't want this baby, I want an abortion I said - he agreed, we weren't in the right place to bring up and have this baby. So, I booked a doctor's appointment (for the next day).

But for that day, I behaved like I was keeping the baby, just in case, I didn't smoke, I didn't drink and I was cautious about what I ate - it was like a little bit of mother nature took over, I can't explain it, but I looked after my body and the baby, even though I didn't want to keep it.

I went to the doctors the next morning, scared and alone and I explained the situation - she was understanding and nonjudgmental and needed to confirm the pregnancy and just check me over, I pee'd in a pot and she confirmed I was pregnant, then she wanted to feel my tummy and that was when it all changed again, yes I knew I was pregnant but what she said next threw me into panic, she could feel the baby, up high near my tummy button, this indicated to her that I was around 5 months pregnant - 5 months?! How?!

She insisted that I went for a scan that night, as if I didn't want to keep the baby, I had to move fast, I went back to the office, completely shell shocked and had to break the news to him, he wanted to come with me to the hospital, but the only place with an appointment that night was an hour drive away.

Stressed and panicking - all I could think was how on earth will I cope with a baby!!

The drive to the hospital was awkward and silent, neither of us knew what to say, so we said nothing. The staff at the hospital were amazing, so lovely, they knew the situation and when they laid me down for the scan they turned the screen away as they knew what we wanted.

But that moment was the defining point in my life, I can still picture it like it was yesterday - I was told that I was 24 weeks and 5 days pregnant, the legal abortion limit was 25 weeks, I basically had 48 hours until the limit was up.

It was too late, far too late, I couldn't do that - the baby was a person, a human, someone who had kept hidden from me, that hadn't given any signs she was there until now and it was too late she's was coming, this baby had kept hidden long enough to be born.

I asked them to turn the screen around so I could see my baby and there she was a huge baby on the screen, a fully developed baby, inside my tummy that even to this day I have no idea where she could possibly have been hiding!! I didn't look pregnant at all (she was nearly 8lb when she was born!!).

Everything changed, there and then and even to this day I am so very grateful for my beautiful daughter who is now 18 and I do not regret having for a single second, she has, alongside her sister, enhanced my life and made me who I am today, everything I have done since that day, everything I do and everything I will ever do is for them.

The drive home was uncomfortable.

The next few months were a whirlwind and can only be described as crazy busy, we had to tell people, work, family and friends, and wait, excitedly for her arrival, which she was 2 weeks late, which is the story of her life, she's still late for everything now!!!

A year later I had another daughter, who didn't have quite as an exciting entrance in this world, but equally as meaningful. Sadly, the relationship broke down, despite our best efforts.

I found myself living in what we cutely nicknamed 'The Dolls House' a cute but quite small 2 bedroom terrace, but it was all me and my girls needed. By this point they were 3 and 4 and both at pre-school, so I went and found myself a little job, it wasn't what I enjoyed but it paid the rent on our house and the bills, although it didn't always stretch to cover everything, I spent a lot of my time juggling which bill was more important - my parents were amazing and always did what they could for me and the girls and always bought us food.

When my eldest daughter started school, I had to change jobs as I couldn't afford to pay for childcare and work, so I got a job working weekends and evenings in a local call centre, as a customer service advisor, I worked when the girls stayed with their dad, it worked perfectly.

But as time went on I realised I had no room for anything other than the girls and working.

I then met someone new and after a while, we moved in together and I was able to give up the job that took me away at weekends and evenings, but I needed something, I'm not a person who can sit at home doing nothing...but what could I do.....I made a list of all of the things I loved doing, which oddly seems to be all the things other people don't like doing! For example, I love and I mean LOVE spreadsheets!!

One afternoon whilst sat in the hairdressers, as I was waiting for my highlights to take I was flicking through a magazine, an article caught my attention, it was about a lovely lady who looked bright and happy and how she had lost lots of weight, but it wasn't her weight loss that captured my attention, it was her job.

This lady worked as a VA, something I had never heard of, she helped small business owners online with all of their admin - a freelance PA / Administrator. The more I read the more I knew, this was it, this was what I had been looking for, this was my answer.

I set about researching what a VA was, what they did and how I should start, my boyfriend at the time thought it was a fantastic idea and we paid a friend of his to build me a website - it was a very basic site, but I had a website and a logo and then all I needed was clients, but I had no idea how to get them!

I always find it fascinating as to why people name their companies what they do, mine has a story behind it too - so it's apt that I include this here.

When I set up the company, I spent days trying to think of names, no easy feat! At the time I was obsessed with a tv series called Firefly - this series had a spin-off movie which they called Serenity (the space ship in the series was called Serenity) as soon as I heard that name, I knew I wanted to incorporate it within the business, then I thought about my ideal client and what they needed, my ideal client was someone who worked hard, too hard and never has time to relax, so I thought about words that went with serenity, then it hit me, my ideal client was seeking the serenity in their business - and Seeking Serenity was born!

Facebook was just beginning to build momentum back then and I found an online group to join, it was a lady who was also a VA and she gave lots of brilliant advice, she had built up her business from scratch whilst travelling the world.

One day this lady announced she was going to start coaching VA's and she needed 6 people to be her BETA testers for a 12-week course - we had to apply with our details and why we should be her BETA tester. She had hundreds of people apply for the course, but I believed deep down that I had a place, I kept telling myself it was mine (I hadn't discovered the Law of Attraction back then).

I can still remember the moment she announced the winners, I had my PC on in my study at home, stood in the doorway watching her do her live video, half in half out, my heart was pounding, one by one she called out the names and then....she said my name, I was ecstatic, over the moon, so much so I think I cried, I ran around the house screaming with delight!

I was so excited and so full of enthusiasm.

That course changed everything for me, we had our websites re-built, new professional branding, we had 1:1 calls and 12 weeks of online coaching, to which we STILL have access to now, I am truly grateful for her and her training course.

I've been lucky enough to work with some incredible people over the years, I've watched and supported several people grow from new startups to fully fledged business owners with a team of people, and sometimes life gives you an opportunity that you have to pinch yourself over!

Mine was about 5 years ago, I started working with a new client, they were a team of people and they'd got quite busy, so they needed some support, with some techy aspects. During our initial meeting, they said they had a couple of high profile clients that I would probably be working with, they wanted me 1 day a week on-site in their offices in central London, which I was ok with because working in London was a novelty!

One morning, I was sat at my desk working away and in they walked, the 'high profile' client was a very high profile boyband - I was taken aback as they walked in like they owned the place, they knew everyone, they greeted me like they'd known me for years - I tried my hardest to act cool (I'll never know if I did or not!!)

I was so excited when I was told that I'd be doing some work online for this band and I'd have to work closely with them, their manager and their PA.

I loved the time that I worked with them, I even managed to get tickets (not just any tickets, I got VIP backstage tickets) for one of their concerts, I took a friend who had been a huge fan, and then I took her backstage and introduced her to them, she stood there with her mouth open unable to speak!!

I am a little bit of a geek at heart, I love a good piece of tech, my phone, tablet and laptop are my best friends, I have an app for everything and all of them are synced - I love being organised and have some great apps that help me to organise my work and life.

I love tinkering with apps, learning how to do new things online - which is why I am a techy VA!

My love of tech probably started when I met my ex-husband, who was a professional geek (his words, not mine, I tried to get them to put that on our marriage certificate but they wouldn't!!).

Everything in our house was set up in a way that meant I had to learn to understand coding (I can't code, but I can work out what it means).

Not long after starting out as a VA I realised there was a gap in the market for networking groups solely for mums, I wanted to create somewhere where people like me, a mum at home with small children, could come along and network with other mum business owners AND bring their children too.

I set up a facebook group and hoped for the best, back then, there were no facebook ads so it was a case of inviting the few mums I knew and then hope that it would grow.

I was amazed, at first it was the odd person here and there, then more and more mums joined my groups, within 6 months I had nearly 1000 mums that had joined us.

I soon had to ask for help moderating, so many people needed so much help, so I asked an old school friend of mine who ran her own business and another friend who I used to work with - the 3 of us began to organise the group - a photographer friend loaned his studio for one afternoon so we could have a local meet up.

It was amazing, we had cakes made, balloons and the local paper came, along with around 50 mums and their children.

The group grew and we started having regular meetings and event, we even managed to get a slot at a really big local show, where we had a tent full of mums and their products - I was so proud of what I had created.

I set up the networking group as a free group to help other mums, and whilst it was brilliant and I made lots of new friends and contacts, it wasn't making any money but was taking up a lot of my spare time, despite having a little team of helpers.

I had to make the decision to move on and focus on my VA business, so I sold my little group to a lovely lady who also ran a networking group locally for mums (lots had started to pop up since I started mine) and she merged them together.

I still have fond memories of that time, and I have a glass engraved bottle with the group logo on that one of the mums made me.

2018 was my Annus horribilis, which is Latin for a horrible year, it was a year that most of me would like to put a line under and forget, but at the same time, I met the most wonderful person who I now share my life with!

November 2017 saw me walk away from my marriage and 12 years, after trying hard for several years to make it work, which had already started to take its toll on my business. I had to move out of my home, the one I had lived in for 8 years, the one that saw my children grow up and I also had to leave one of my dogs behind - we had 2 and we took one each, anyone who knows me knows how much my dogs mean to me and I felt like she'd died the day I left, she looked at me out of the window and I drove away sobbing, it still breaks my heart I don't see her every day.

Divorce is an unpleasant and highly stressful situation to find yourself in, you end up dragging up details about each other that you didn't need to know, but the authorities insist on you doing, you have to point the blame at each other to end things legally, at the time of writing this the law has just changed and you no longer have to do this, which is brilliant, there is no need to hurt each other more than necessary.

I hated being single, I was so lonely, I felt like I needed someone and quickly became obsessed with Tinder and Plenty of fish, it became a full-time job, I clearly needed something to occupy my mind and distract me from being lonely.

My business began to suffer, every time I turned on the laptop the anxiety rose within me and I'd soon go back to my online dating world, where I could be someone else and forget all the shit going on in the background.

But, I had money from my divorce, I was ok for now, I joined lots of paid for groups, coaching and courses, these things were merely plasters for my business, I didn't need them, they weren't helping me, if anything they were having a detrimental effect on me and my business. I discovered that a lot of people online sadly under deliver on their promises.

I also bought a flash new car, got hair extensions and botox - it was all moments of feeling good about myself, but these moments were gone in a flash.

What I really needed was to learn to love myself again, to work on my mindset and realise I was enough, just me.

In September 2018 I had had enough of the online world,

poor decisions, poor mindset and a year that I wanted to erase had taken its toll, I thought the grass would be greener on the other side and went back to working in an office 9-5. The first week was great, I enjoyed meeting people, I enjoyed turning up at 9 and leaving at 5. But after that I realised I'd made a huge mistake, office life wasn't for me and I needed to get a grip, kick myself up the bottom and get back to online working.

So I set about building my website, something that I find so easy, so relaxing and so satisfying, I rejoined the online communities and started to network within the industry - I joined online groups and started to learn, something I am so passionate about, being a VA means staying at the top of the game, knowing how to do anything and everything.

I then re-found Tiffany, someone I had met in person back in 2018 on a business retreat and started watching her online again, chatting with her and spoke to her about the last year, she helped me immensely, she started coaching me. I recreated my morning routine, I dusted off my gratitude book and I started to journal my feelings and issues away. I found that by writing it down, getting it all off of my chest I was able to draw a line under the things and people that had hurt me in the last year.

My morning routine now consists of:

Gratitude - I get my notepad and set my timer for 2 minutes, I then list all of the things I am grateful for and why.

Meditation - I love to listen to a short morning meditation to set me up for the day.

Affirmation cards - I have a deck of affirmation cards and every morning I pull one out and put it on the fridge, so I read it several times a day.

Brain dump - Anything that's going through my head gets dumped on to paper - I then organise this into my to-do list and anything that's bothering me goes into my journal, and I journal out the issues and solutions.

Doing these simple things every morning I have found a huge amount of clarity and focus.

I also found that writing a simple letter to the person that hurt you in the past really helps, writing to them, telling them how they hurt you, how it made you feel and that you forgive them - then burn it - let it go and move on. The feeling you get letting go is immense.

With the guidance of the right people around me, my business has grown in leaps and bounds, every day it continues to grow.

I eventually met someone online, who actually wasn't the kind of guy I thought I wanted, firstly he's a few years younger than me, something I never thought I'd want - he's also not from my hometown, which meant that I've learned to move away from where I have lived and breathed for over 40 years and I've discovered I'm ok with that. I stepped out of my comfort zone and found someone I want to be with for a very long time, we're over a year into our relationship now and he's supporting me and my business in ways nobody else ever had, he's the reason I'm here writing this now, when I told him about this book his reply was, just do it, you do so much for everyone else it's time to do something for you.

When I restarted my VA business after my bad few years I was really scared, I was worried that people wouldn't take me seriously, but I couldn't have been more wrong, I feel that everything is lined up and things are moving at a fast pace, I'm confident and happy and positive and I know where I am going.

When things are not going your way, it's very easy to forget the basics, self-love is essential, I'm learning to love myself more, over the years I've spent far too much time putting myself down, putting off doing that live video, because I'm a little overweight and my voice sounds half posh and half common all at the same time, or not having professional photos taken because I'm worried about my teeth not being straight enough or my eyebrows need shaping, at the end of the day though nobody is going to judge you on how you look, everyone has their own worries and concerns about the way they look. So, something we all, myself included need to know, is to jump right in, countdown from 5 and just do it.

I've set myself a goal this year to seize every opportunity that comes my way and if it scares me, even better.

Amazing things happen on the other side of your comfort zone.

I'm a huge believer in the law of attraction, goal lists and visual goal boards, a few years ago I created a goal board, it's great to sit there, dream about the things you want to achieve, places you want to go and things you want.

One of the items on my goal board was a picture of Mykonos, I had no idea where in Mykonos it was, but it was a place I really wanted to go (on my travel wish list). A few months later, in a group I was in online a post popped up about a business retreat to Mykonos, I knew there and then I had to go. One evening, in Mykonos on the business retreat, we'd all been out in the town for something to eat and someone suggested watching the sunset over the ocean, we headed to the sea, we walked around the corner and there it was, the exact image from my vision board, not only had I made it to Mykonos, I had actually walked to exactly where the picture was taken, I was lost for words, I, of course, shared it with everyone with me!

As business owners people spend far too much time, time that they're not making money, tinkering with things they are not confident with or they don't enjoy doing.

A landing page, for example, would take me a couple of hours to put together, sync up with a newsletter list and add content, but people spend hours, even days fiddling with little bits, flicking back and forth to YouTube trying to work out how to do a single tweak.

Facebook ads are an area that people struggle with, I was talking to my coach about this not long ago, when she suggested that I should be helping people with their ads, my response was, but they're so easy to do, but after some market research I realised that business owners really struggle with them.

Don't struggle with tasks within your business, spend time doing what you're amazing at and then outsource to someone, such as a VA who can easily deal with it saving you money and time.

A list of edits on a WordPress website would take me an hour, maybe 2 depending on how much there was to do, but some people might try and save some money and learn it themselves and then take all day doing it - whilst they might get the satisfaction of having done it themselves, they could have spent that day doing a webinar or Facebook live and then bringing in a new client.

Working as a Virtual Assistant has suited me and my life perfectly, I work doing the things that light my soul and I get to be with my children when they need me.

My daughter said to me a few years ago, mum, I've never appreciated what you have done for us, you've always been there for us, no matter what, if we're sick, you've come and got us from school and sat with us on the sofa with your laptop.

Little things like that make all the hard work working for myself, worth it.

I'm now working with my boyfriend renovating a house we have together, I can multitask, I can work on client work and the house renovation at the same time.

JO BOSWELL | 225

No matter what direction life pulls you in, we all have the ability to turn ourselves back around and be stronger than before.

I am rising like a phoenix from the ashes, positive thinking only, driving my life and my business in the right direction.

Watch out world, I'm here and it's my time.

ABOUT THE AUTHOR

JO BOSWELL

Jo Boswell is a warm loving entrepreneur, who cannot do enough to help people and gets genuine happiness from seeing her client's businesses grow.

Working as a Virtual Assistant for the last 11 years, Jo has juggled being a single mum twice to her 2 daughters who are now 17 and 18. Jo prides herself that she has always been there for her girls, she has never missed any of the important moments of them growing up.

She first discovered the rewarding work of being a virtual assistant (VA) back in 2008, when she was attempting to perfect the art of juggling mummy duties with work, realising that childcare would almost exceed her income. One day, while sat in the hairdressers, she flicked through a magazine and an interesting article about a woman who worked as a VA jumped out at her, everything about that article resonated with her.

She was then lucky enough to win a place on a training academy for new VAs which taught her the basics of what she needed to get up and running

Jo loves helping female entrepreneurs with all of the tasks that they don't enjoy or take up too much or their valuable time to learn, she is always the 'mum' in every situation, business or pleasure.

When she's not working Jo loves spending time with her daughters, her 3 dogs and she also loves to travel and specifically enjoys snowboarding, and being able to lie in the sun in a hot country.

CONTACT

EMAIL jo@joboswell.com

WEBSITE   https://joboswell.com/   www.seekingserenityva.com

LINKEDIN https://www.linkedin.com/in/joboswell/

facebook.com/jolboswell

instagram.com/missjoboss

10

KAYLIE DOLLISON

*1*989 - I was born in the middle of a snowy February Friday night in a small town in Texas. My mom was 18, and I clearly have no recollection or memory of this event or many of the events to follow.

Over the next 18 years my dad would be a come and go kind of dad, who liked to drink a little more than he liked to be a dad. He was always running off on a new adventure, sending a post card or a letter from wherever he would end up next. He would show up, stay for a while, only to leave again. The summer before I started high-school he'd bring me a trunk full of belongings and leave for Alaska. I wouldn't see him again until 2 months after I graduated high school.

My mom would spend the next 18 years trying to find herself, which left us without that strong mother/daughter bond. This left me spending the majority of my time in my bedroom in my own little world.

1995 - I kissed a boy in my kindergarten class that year and my best friend (nanny/grandma) passed away. She was my person in life up until that moment, and I have more memories with her in the first few years of my life than I do anyone else. I started seeing a school counsellor shortly after she died and didn't stop until middle school. My nanny's passing truly made my tiny world crumble and it made a huge impact on the years to follow.

2001- I started middle school which is basically middle earth but with mean girls and rude boys. It's also where the first, second, and final (third) rumour about me would be birthed.

7th grade first semester - So in case you didn't know, a lot of your class mates start to get boobs about this time, I wasn't one of those, but I did get my first padded bra this year. I remember being on the playground in the 6th grade, and kids standing around me singing "roses are red, violets are black, why is your chest as flat as your back", and now I was getting accused of being a bra stuffer, I couldn't win here. Now thirty-year-old Kaylie knows that violets are purple, you don't need boobs until your grown, and boys are definitely IDIOTS.

This little girl grew up and now understands that because of those non-existent tits and her vagina, she is the most powerful force on the planet. She also learned that padded bras, push up bras, water bras, sometimes duct tape, and make up would be needed to enhance your assets. She also learned that if that failed you could always just go get fake ones....but, at thirteen I wasn't yet wise to all the magical tit ways; so, I cried.

Now I don't know why kids who were twelve/thirteen years old were watching movies like American pie or Road Trip, but some kid's parents let them learn a lot of things way too quickly because of their lack of paying attention. My 2nd round at rumour town came from "that one time at band camp" line and the fact that I too played the flute. So that must have meant I'd go home and use it to masturbate with after school instead of listening to Brittany Spears pretending I was a pop star and playing frogger on my Nintendo.

When people can LIE about you and it hurts you so badly that you cry in front of them, they realize they can say ANYTHING about you and you'll get mad, defensive and probably cry and that means entertainment for them. That means no one looking their way, at their flaws. Some of those kids I went to school with must have been going through some serious shit because it got worse....so much worse.

My mom started dating this guy I didn't particularly care for, and he had a daughter who was my little bothers age, which was about nine at the time. My mom had talked about moving in with him but that would mean me moving schools, and I wasn't too thrilled with that idea at first. But once someone decided to tell my entire 7th grade class that I put peanut butter on my vagina and let my dog lick it off, well... that changed everything! I wanted as far away from that school and from those kids and from those teachers who wouldn't do anything about it, as I could get. So, I told my mom I'd move school and I did.

So, it's 2nd semester of 7th grade, it's the first day back after Christmas break and here I am in a new school. A fresh start! I'm excited. Especially since we had just moved out of Pa's house and into a trailer with this guy my mom had decided to marry, and his daughter who I would be sharing a room with. It was a nice change being in a room with someone rather than being all alone and I finally had the sister I had thought I always wanted.

While I'm sitting in the office waiting on my schedule, I see a boy that had "been my boyfriend" in the 4th grade. You know, we held hands once so obviously we were in love. But he moved, and I hadn't seen him again until he knocked on the window, smiled and waved at me. I just knew this was the change I needed.

It was a small school. I had 100 people in my graduating class and a new kid really got attention. I was loving it! People were talking to me, girls invited me to eat lunch with them, and some boy who didn't even know my name asked if I wanted to be his girlfriend! See, I told you boys were idiots.

I wish I had known then how gossip works and how rumours spread (now keep in mind this was pre cell phones in almost everyone's hand, and a few years before social media so things didn't travel as fast, but they still travelled). Had I have known; I would have never smiled back at my

4th grade crush in that office. I would have kept my head down, kept my nose in a book, and moved along invisible. Because being invisible would have been better than becoming peanut butter girl at a tiny school, in a tiny town.

It only took a few days for that rumour to spread like wild fire, and these kids were relentless! I couldn't walk down a hallway or in a class room without being called peanut butter girl. Boys would ask if I wanted them to bring their dogs over to my house. They would throw trash at me when I got off the school bus. They would call me names at school, on the bus, in my neighbourhood, and they would make crude jokes and comments.

They would ask if I preferred creamy or crunchy, ask if I preferred a certain brand, and they would even bring me jars of peanut butter to school and to my house. I even had my bedroom window knocked out once and I cried EVERY SINGLE DAY. I couldn't understand what I had done to not only have someone make up this LIE about me, but for so many people to actually BELIEVE IT WAS TRUE! For them to continue to tell it over and over, and to add bits and pieces to it along the way. And for them to act as if they weren't ruining a young girl's life.

I was the same as every other 13 year-old girl I knew. I played with barbies with my step sister, I played video games, I sang in the mirror with my microphone hair brush, I read so many books ...but no one cared, and most didn't believe me, or at least didn't want to believe me when I told them it was a lie.

I will forever be thankful for the group of girls who befriended me that first day of school and never allowed that rumour to affect our friendship.

2004 - high school starts which became a literal hell on earth and where this story really starts.....

I hate when people say high school is the best time of your life. High school SUCKS and if you're 60 looking back saying high school was the good ole days and the "time of your life", I feel really sorry for you.

I was probably the most popular girl in my entire school (I didn't even realise that until I sat down to write this chapter). Being popular is about being known, and well I was definitely known. I bet if you ask almost anyone who went to my school who Peanut Butter Girl was they'd have a story to tell you. However, almost every single story would be a horrible lie that NO girl should have to go through and endure for years.

Even years after high-school has ended, I have had to endure the effects of those horrible rumours. Being a 15 year old girl in a school with 15-18 year old boys who think you're letting your dog go to town on your vagina isn't the ideal situation to find yourself in. I knew it would be rough. I thought I had prepared myself, but I didn't know just how bad it would get.

Now as a 15 year old getting alcohol and pot is kinda difficult. Not impossible, but not as easy as it seems in the movies either. It's also a lot harder to do when you live with your parents, are underage and have no job. So, the kids I started smoking weed in the woods with after school, started telling me about pills. And those were so easy to find! My friends had prescriptions for all kinds of things, so I took them.

When a few people started figuring out I was doing pills, they started asking me for some. Well I didn't want to share the good things I had like - Phenergan, hydrocodone, and sleeping pills, so I sold them vitamin E pills instead. And I was doing a good job, until a guy had a reaction and I was caught at school with a prescription that didn't belong to me.

I had found myself not only expelled from school, but sent to alternative school. It was such a strange new world. There were some really bad kids that did some really bad things. And we had to wear white shirts and jeans and tennis shoes and walk on red duct tape. We had a bathroom monitor when we went to the bathroom. We sat in cubicles all by ourselves, with no teacher actually teaching. We just had a room monitor to make sure we stayed quiet, stayed seated, and stayed working. I secretly loved it there. I was this 80-pound, super white girl with short dark brown hair, blue eyes, freckles. I looked and sounded so innocent.

Everyone including the teachers would make comments about how I didn't look like I belonged there, and they thought I was so sweet. I didn't know it was possible to be a popular girl while being in alternative school, but I was. The teachers loved me, the bad boys there really loved me (even though we only got to talk for like 10 minutes before school started), and even the principal loved me. No one knew anything about peanut butter girl, and it was nice. I was actually sad when I had to leave there after three months and go back to school. I think if I had just stayed in alternative school doing my homework every day, things probably would've gone a little differently.

So, I go back to school and the girl whose prescription I had wasn't exactly my biggest fan anymore, and our 3 year friendship was over. Now in case you've never been involved with a group of girls who have to choose one friend over the other, let me just say for the girl who's not chosen, life can get hard. Especially when you relied on that group of friends as a safety net.

January 11, 2004 - I've been back to school for about a week. Rumours about how I was mad at the girl whose prescription I'd had spread like wild fire. I'm sure she assumed I blamed her, but I didn't. Rumours spread that I was sleeping with the guys and girls I was in alternative school with also circulated. And, who could forget peanut butter girl!

I ate lunch in the band-hall hallway a lot that year. They used to leave the doors unlocked during lunch so we could go practice and some of the other band kids just hung out down there. It was my safe place, or at least it was. Until one lunch period I found myself alone in the hallway with a senior boy.

He kept making comments about how he could do things a

236 | WHEN SHE RISES

dog couldn't, and I just needed to feel what a man could do. Now standing at under 5 foot, I'm sure at the time seeing how I'm only 5'2 now, a 6+ foot tall jock blocking your way, saying awful things to you, is terrifying and what do you know, I started crying. If you learn nothing from this book remember this.... DON'T CRY IN FRONT OF PEOPLE WHO HURT YOU!! Even if you are not tough, pretend you are! That saying "fake it till you make it" applies to many different situations you will find yourself in.

He grabbed my wrist, told me not to say a word, and took me to one of the back practice rooms. He put a chair under the door knob, while still holding my arm. He turned me around, put his arm under my arm pit and around my neck to hold me still. He put his hand over my mouth, bent me over a music stand, and raped me. When he was done, he told me not to tell a soul because he could ruin my life, and no one would believe me anyway. He was right. The one person I told said "there is no way ($;$/) did that he's not that kind of guy. "Maybe you just want a guy to have sex with you so people will stop making jokes about dogs." I've never told another soul that story.

Well until now when my husband and parents and friends will be reading this. Some may blame themselves. Some will wish they could go back and change things, done things or said things differently. But you can't. You can't do anything. I can't do anything. All we can do is share our stories that may be similar with each other, with our sons our daughters and enforce an open line of communication that works for ALL subjects and opinions. And most importantly, LISTEN even when it is hard.

For the next 3 years, I'd find myself in a fist fight, more depressed than I have ever been, praying that I would just die, dating guys way too old for me, and pregnant by the guy I started dating at the end of my sophomore year and thought I'd be with forever, always, and a day. But that actually only turned out to be about four years and finally finding out my step dad was cheating on my mom.

Life sure has a funny way of showing you exactly what you need, exactly when you need it! I wanted to be a mom. I wanted to start a family. I wanted unconditional love with everything inside me. So, getting pregnant at 17 was terrifying, but also exciting. Before I got pregnant, I had no plans for life after graduation. I knew I had to graduate so I wouldn't disappoint my Grandpa, but I hadn't given a thought to what happens next.

I know that in life you have check marks along the way that help guide you down the path, but what was a girl with a 2.0 GPA and zero self-worth and confidence going do in collage? I knew if I drove my car off a bridge or successfully took enough pills to not wake up Pa would be devastated, and I couldn't put him through that. I was working at Walmart and knew I didn't want a future in retail. The problem was I didn't see a future at all.

A baby made a plan, a next step. So, I leaped and moved out the day after my high school graduation with the boy I had been dating since my sophomore year and was having a baby and starting a family with. I did this not knowing that a year later I would find myself a single mom, on a wild ride into another round of depression and many regretful nights. The next few months I'd find myself living with friends, drinking a lot more than anyone around me knew, and really losing myself. I can't even tell you all the stupid things I did. And then I met a boy name Eric.

Now at first, I wanted nothing to do with him, when I heard about his past and I certainly didn't need to add any more problems to my already messed up life. I told my friends not to introduce us. I'm pretty sure the words "do not bring that stupid kid to my apartment" where used and at our first meeting I was not thrilled by the fact that he liked my butt.

However, I found myself falling quickly in love with him; consumed with this overwhelming feeling that this boy would change my life. I married him six months after the day we met. And while we have had many ups and down and moments where life has really knocked us down and made us question many things, our love for one another has been the biggest strength in both of our lives these last 11 years.

Where one of us is lacking, the other is strong. In all areas of our life together, we make the perfect team because we are so different. We saved each other. Eric has always supported me in every crazy idea that I have come up with. Like when we were engaged, and I told him MTV had sent me an email and wanted to interview us to be on Engaged and Underage.

They sent a camera crew out to follow us around for a few days, and he went right along with it. There was also the year I spent turning our house into a dog rescue home because I wanted to make a difference in the world. I don't know many men who would stay with someone who wanted to keep 27 dogs at their house while she found them families to love them, but he did! And in that year I found countless dogs new homes.

Then there was another time I wanted to audition for the Singing Bee on CMT.....and did he tell me I was crazy? Nope he drove me 2.5 hours away to the audition. And when I made it, he supported me flying to L.A all alone, to be on a TV show because that's what I wanted to do.

I spent the first 6 years of our marriage as a full time stay at home mom. I had a random job here and there as a waitress, a secretary for an attorney, a night auditor at a hotel, and as a personal assistant when things got tough. But they never lasted long because I'd rather be home broke with my babies. I played around with a few direct sales jobs that didn't get me anywhere until 2015 when I found one I became obsessed with.

The products were great and the affordability of it excited me because me, Eric, our three kids and two dogs were living with Pa. After selling our house we had outgrown (our 3 bedroom single wide trailer), we needed something bigger, so moving in with Pa and saving for a house was our plan.

It was my 4th pregnancy that really change my business and my life. I have never worked or prayed harder than I did those 9 months. I mean I was prepared for Pa to tell us we need to move out right then. I prepared myself for it, I prepared Eric for it. I knew the possibility that that could happen was real and it terrified me. I went back to Pa's room where he was lying in bed watching NCIS and told him not to be mad, but I was pregnant. He told me that we should probably just stop looking for a house and plan to stay here because we couldn't afford anything bigger than his house and he had plenty of room. I was stunned, shocked, relieved and overjoyed all in the same 30 seconds.

They announced an incentive trip to go to Italy in that little direct sales business I'd fell in love with, and to be honest, I didn't think I stood a chance. But I started praying about it constantly. Every waking moment I thought about it in one way or another. I was making Facebook live videos about the products. I was wearing branded clothing from the business.

The excitement I felt was so real, and the closer I got to earning that trip and realising it was possible, the harder I pushed. It was so crazy to watch all these people following me on social media and instead of joining me and trying to earn their own ticket to go on this incredible trip, they were helping me. People were sharing my post, and they were sharing my videos. People genuinely wanted me to go on this trip.

It sounds crazy when I say that you can feel so much love through social media, but let me tell you, you can feel the love when people are staying up until midnight watching you try to hit promotions or earn a free trip. Even when it has ZERO effect on their life. Often, I would find myself so overwhelmed with emotions of happiness, joy, support and love that I would just cry. People would stop me and tell me that I was glowing from pregnancy, but I think it was so much more than pregnancy. I think it was this feeling like people cared, like I was somebody finally worth caring about. I earned that trip to Italy and I worked my ass off for it. And while I was there, I enjoyed every single moment.

I was 6 months pregnant with my 4th child standing in Rome and couldn't believe this was really my life. When we first arrived, we went to a roof top to look over the city. It was there on that roof top that my life started to change. I rode in a gondola in Venice. I bought a Louis Vuitton bag in Florence.

I had the most amazing ride in a carriage tied to a bike playing loud music and being driven through the streets with one of my best friends while our driver was yelling and telling everyone we were princesses. I cried while walking through the Colosseum because all I could think about while walking down those halls, were all the times I felt worthless. All the times I thought about ending my life.

Every moment I'd let someone else decide my worth and my value.

I cried because I knew I would never again be the same girl. I left so much of myself down there in the coliseum, all my guilt and all my shame stayed behind. And for the first time in my life, I felt free. I learned so much about myself on that trip. I learned how powerful I was. I learned how influential I was, and I learned that my voice could be used for so many things.

So, I came home determined to change my life, my family's life, and as many people's lives around me that I could. I started taking classes, listening to podcasts, reading books, watching webinars - doing everything I could to rise up. For the last nine months I had been working as a spray tanner in a local salon, but I knew that wasn't something I could do long term, because I had a vision. A vision of more. A vision my husband supported full force. A vision that would quickly turn into a reality, when he finally gave me the push I needed to go be successful on my own.

I get asked all the time "oh you just do spray tans?". As if I need another niche in my life to be considered successful.

Well technically, yes, I just do spray tans, but absolutely no.

I get to see woman and men in the most vulnerable positions which has to have a certain trust behind it.

Those secret hidden tattoos from early years.

The scars left from abuse from a loved one and some from self-harm.

I watch and listen as both young girls and grown women feel the insecurities wash over them as they start to notice every flaw, stretch mark, or scar I may notice but never do until they point them out.

I listen to happy moments, proud moments, hard and sad moments, and sometimes devastating ones as well.

I know about pregnancy before most husbands. I get to watch girls grow up into amazing women, and tan them all along their life journeys. For a short time each week, I get to be a bright light - a smile, and a friend to those who enter my door. So, yea, I am a spray tanner! But I am really so much more.

I am my hardest critic sometimes. I have an old bad habit of comparing my success, my happiness, and everything else with those around me. Even writing this book, I wonder how me, and my story will compare to the amazing woman I'm in collaboration with. These are big shoes to fill and to follow. Self-doubt was another big issue I've always dealt with and still do, more often than I like to admit. I'm always terrified to do big things because it's always in the back of my mind that someone will bring up those three little words that still send a shiver of terror up my spine "peanut butter girl". How funny is that?

I am this badass boss of a mom and business owner/woman empowerer, and yet, I am still terrified. I am terrified that when the day comes that I decide to run for state representative or president of the United States, or anything BIG in life like THIS BOOK, I get nervous that my past will hold me back.

I think that is part of our problem in life; the constant comparison to those around us when all we should be comparing ourselves to is the us of our past. Am I better than I was then? Am I stronger now? Am I wiser now? HECK YES I AM!!! I'm pretty sure Eric would punch anyone who said anything bad about me right in the face, and it wouldn't be the first time.

A tragedy is a tragedy. And it's so easy to say and think that what others went through may be worse than what I went through, somehow making our pain seem less than theirs, but one tragedy doesn't trump another. Your hurt, your pain, your losses are yours. And what you go through, how you deal and heal, is completely different from the person beside you. Don't compare your tragedy with others. We live in a world where we can create ourselves, even reinvent ourselves. A lot of people do it yearly, at the start of a new year. But, I do it daily. Each day I try to be the most positive, most kind version of myself. Do I fail? Yes, often! But if I can strive each day to be better than yesterday, despite the setbacks, I'm becoming a better me all along the way.

It wasn't until I sat down and thought about what I really wanted out of life, what would fulfil every area of my soul, when I thought about what I, Kaylie Paige Dollison, wanted out of life in order to be TRULY happy, did everything start to fall into place. Success for me is knowing that I created an entire prospering business and entire brand! It's knowing that I have raised KIND children in a world that is far from kind. It's knowing I have a man beside me holding my hand and encouraging me every step of the way, even on the days I doubt myself. It's knowing that every day for the rest of Pa's life, me, Eric and our kids will be here...right here in this house living and doing life together with Pa the way Jesus wanted us to.

Every single experience has been or will be a LESSON.

Whatever you learn from it will either help you or help someone else, and both are equally as important.

You cannot hate the things that have helped shaped the person you are, or the person you are becoming because each event, experience, circumstance, relationship, moment has made you, YOU.

Eric's encouragement, support and belief in me has been a driving force behind all of my success. I think Eric is the first person to ever believe in me. He's dang sure the first person to ever push and encourage me to fulfill a dream. But the thing is, Eric believed in me the entire time. It wasn't until I started to believe in myself that the magic really started to happen.

My biggest asset to my business, marriage, friendship, life, success, has simply been, to be me. The more I shared of myself and who I was authentically, the more I attracted my ideal clients. Because YES, I have an ideal client! I can honestly and fully say I adore and love each client I have! I do happy dances when most book their appointments, because it means good conversations with people I value. And isn't that what doing life with others is all about?

I could have allowed my past to consume me, to surround myself with nothing but the darkness that enveloped me for so long but being a light in a dark world is better. Showing others my strength has allowed them to find some of their own. Showing others it's okay to be your weird, strange, silly, crazy self has been a big part of my legacy over the last few years, I hope that legacy continues to grow to show women everywhere they hold the power and key to their future.

The only person who can ever change your life is YOU.

You can surround yourself with those who motivate you, you can be set up on a good path, you can be lead the way, you can be shown how, you can have all the knowledge to better your life, but the only way to actually do it is by getting up and taking the initiative into making it happen. No one can do it for you, it has to be you.

When I look back at everything I have overcome, how every mistake of my past doesn't define who I am today, and how much I have grown in every area in life, I am sometimes in utter disbelief. I've been told for years how inspiring I am, but I didn't really realise it until I sat down and started writing this chapter. Thinking back about my past has wrecked me time and time again over the last few weeks. But I would never have become the woman I am today with the compassion, heart and want to help others without being that girl first.

Without knowing and experiencing that pain I wouldn't be able to understand hurt, pain, loss, depression, sadness the way I do today. When YOU start to believe in YOU your world will start to change. Your focus will shift, your thoughts will change. Over the last 5 years I have built as many women up as I possibly can. I encourage their side hustle, help with their business ventures, shown them that eating that cosmic brownie in bed at 11pm on a Monday night is totally okay!

Girls in domestic violence relationships know they can call me and simply say they want a turkey sandwich and I know that means they need help, and I will do everything I possibly can to help get them safe and that self care is not only not selfish it's a basic necessity that every girl, everyone should be practicing! Say it with me ladies SELF CARE IS NOT SELFISH!!! Everything you want out of life starts with you and your willingness to work hard to make that life a reality.

Your past no matter how messy, ugly, boring or lacking your past is, IT DOES NOT DEFINE YOU! When you start to believe in you, others around you will start believing in you also. On your bad days you'll have their belief in you to help you ride out the storm, and on their bad days your belief in you will have to be enough to pull you through. You are the author, creator, boss of your own life, of your emotions and how you allow outside forces to dictate what will set up a path for you. If I have learned anything in my 30 years on this earth, it's that people will disappoint you time and time again, and that not everyone has the same heart I do. And that's OKAY! Not everyone is meant to understand my journey, and that's okay too. The important part is that I understand it.

If you're reading this book and you're waiting for a sign to change your life, let this be it! Let this be the moment you decide to do whatever makes you happy, to find what makes your heart happy. Find something you can fall utterly and passionately in love with and then DO IT! Go be the kindest, most empathetic, understanding, uplifting version of you that you possibly can, and let that be your legacy. You have ONE shot here in this life to make the most of out of every single moment you are blessed with. So, go make the most out of each moment starting RIGHT NOW and pray every step of the way, because life is a beautiful serendipitous adventure.

ABOUT THE AUTHOR

KAYLIE DOLLISON

Coming from the part of Texas you drive through, not thrive in, Kaylie refused to settle for what would have been the easy way. Her life is one with real adventures and experiences. Dreams, that for most of us are mere passing thoughts of the impossible. Combine her relentless desire to achieve dreams with the sweetness of her soul and wonder truly spills out all around her.

Here she is with a platform to inspire other young women in the most profound way and a humbleness that most wouldn't have in her position.

You can reach her via:

Email: mermaidlagoonspraytanning@gmail.com

f facebook.com/kayliepaigedollison

instagram.com/kaylie_mermaidlagoon

11

KERRY BEAVIS

"*ive yourself your blessing to live a life rich in what you truly desire. Breathe and move forward into who you are meant to be in this universe. Stop playing small and living in fear, you're meant to shine bright with your greatness.*"

When you know there is more....

Have you ever thought that you can achieve so much more than you have, or there is so much more out there that you want to experience, do and have?

You know you deserve more; you know that the "more" that you crave is out there, you just do not know how you will get it.

I am asking you to trust and believe in yourself and the universe a lot more than what you give yourself credit for. You can ACHIEVE what you want, and you most certainly DESERVE what you want. You have got this. I promise.

I have always wanted more. Not in a way that I wasn't grateful for what I had already in my life, and nor was I forever seeking out the next thrill, promotion, hobby. But I knew I was destined to really live out my true desires.

This chapter is my story on how I have risen to be the person I am meant to be in this life experience.

At High School I was bullied. As an only child I was pretty quiet, too nervous to speak up, way too skinny and with a mass of hidden curls. I just wanted to fit in with my new school friends, and for whatever reason I was the target of one girl who excluded me, belittled me and I allowed her actions to affect me so much, that it removed any shred of confidence I had in who I was. The anxiety could be crippling to the point I was sick. I even remember purposely burning my hand on a lightbulb, thinking I could get the day off school the following day. I became a shadow of who I was meant to be. It was a quiet, clever kind of bullying that probably no-one would have known was going on. I did. I remember.

It didn't even go on for long, I spoke out, it got dealt with in the awkward way bullying got dealt with in the 90's, which was humiliating and mortifying. However, I allowed her actions to impose on me for years. And I mean years. The feelings died down, but simmered slightly under the surface, until certain triggers would rev the engine on the self-doubt thoughts, that I was not enough just being me. I was suffocated in my own shitty thoughts and false beliefs.

I became a people pleaser and would (and often still do) retreat from certain big social situations. The child bully victim would hide her head and sink down in to her quiet, happy place just observing. Being an observer means you cannot get hurt. It's much safer. Or so I thought.

Over the years as Patrick Swayze said...no body puts Baby in the corner, I have realised that her actions came from a place in her, where she needed control and to have power as for whatever reason she was lacking in her home life. I have forgiven and I am working on forgetting those last few fragments.

We cannot allow someone else's actions toward us hold so much power that we shrink back, from what we desire. That we stop becoming who we are destined to be, simply because someone else makes us feel not worthy, through their own insecurities or even jealousy.

LIFE LESSON #1

It is not safer to just be an observer in life. It fills me with great sadness that I was just watching and not being free and open to who I was. One thing that this entrepreneurial journey has taught me is that you cannot be quite if you want to succeed. You have to be your biggest cheerleader in order to get to where you want to go. It doesn't mean you have to turn into the loudest person in the room if you are naturally an introvert. Please embrace that....but you have to gain self-acceptance and peace with you are. Who you are right now is ENOUGH!

I made a pact to myself, that I will not allow another human to stop me from shining in my life experience. Chances are, they saw you out shining them and wanted to dull your sparkle. Your radiance tends to just highlight their own self-doubt and lack of self-belief.

When thoughts become things....

The whole bullying event seemed to make me very determined to prove her wrong and that I was destined for big things. It wasn't until I left school that I felt completely free to be me and just go with what my heart said.

It wasn't until years later of still discovering who I was and what I was meant to be doing that I discovered The Law of Attraction.

My first experience of The Law Of Attraction was watching The Secret round a friend's house in my mid 20's. Thoughts become things, who knew! It just seemed to make so much sense.

You sit in traffic, you dwell on it, you get grumpy about it, the morning gets worse, you get madder, you curse everyone, the afternoon is even more horrendous and everything that could go wrong does; technology is not your friend, a client at work wants everything done yesterday, it rains on the way back to the car, oh more traffic, more cursing, more head shaking and tutting, a big bill to open when you get home, burnt dinner and then the cherry on the cake you can't get to sleep because you're still so mad about the day you just had. I feel pretty bummed just imagining it!

But, imagine being grateful for that car journey. Just changing your energy towards the same event can actually be life changing, who wants anger and stress in their life? That journey allows you some quite time before work to listen to your favourite music, catch up with friends, start that audiobook that you brought ages ago, listen to some motivational videos, recite your affirmations or even visualise your goals and desires. Standstill traffic is out of your control, but how you deal with it isn't.

I try to implement LOA into my everyday life and if you focus on the right things, watch your thoughts, be mindful of what you say and take ACTION. Amazing things can happen!

Throughout my career in the beauty industry, I always kept the bigger picture in my minds view. This meant every job I had, had a reason behind it. They were simply stepping stones to get me to the top. I pretty much knew how long I would stay at a place before I had even started. I was a loyal employee, as in I would go over and above what was expected of me BUT I always knew I was going to leave.

One of my career goals was to win Professional Beauty Therapist of The Year. I never felt really ready, not quite in the place both career or even my mindset. But one year I decided I was going to up level and just do it.

That is when the magic really happens, when you decide whole-heartedly that you are going to achieve something. Something deep inside is triggered. You become determined and disciplined to do whatever it takes to make that thing happen.

Will power alone is not enough, just as relying on the Law of Attraction is not enough. Action makes things happen. Inspired action is what makes the difference.

So, I took risks, I invested to make my therapy business premium and the best it could be. I thought like, and I acted as the award winner I wanted to become. I stepped up, to be the person I wanted to be, that could win the title of being the best.

When I told some fellow therapists that I was going to enter the awards, their words were far from encouraging. In fact, they said how hard it was to get through and their glances were enough to think that they believed I could not do it. I could have let their words of doubt stop me, put self-doubt back into the forefront of my view, allowed those word to ring true and stop me from moving forwards to my true desires. But, hands up, I am competitive, and I wanted to prove them wrong! My ego was not going to back down.

LIFE LESSON #2

Peoples opinions are not your concern. People that shut your dreams down only say it from a place of protection as they try to pass their fears and perceptions onto you. But it is up to you to step up, and only listen to your inner voice. Your intuition. That is the only opinion that matters.

So, I applied and answered the questions from my heart and trusted the process.

The best thing I did was not to listen to the doubters, because you know what I was shortlisted as a finalist. Out of 1000's of entries little ol' me that in essence ran a beauty business from a converted bedroom was in the final 6.

This only made me MORE determined to win this accolade. I envisioned my acceptance speech; I wrote down EVERY night that it was my goal to win. I imagined how I would feel, what opportunities would open up, I did every treatment as though the judges were watching me. In my mind I was going to win. I had no room in my head to think otherwise. I could not afford to.

After the finalists were announced we were to go to London for a trades test. Great. The day before I found out I was pregnant. Although planned, I kind of had talked myself out of having a baby right now as I felt it was not a good idea at this time in our lives. The universe thought differently! So, on a cold November off I trotted to The London College of Beauty Therapy with morning sickness, nerves, tummy cramps, a case full of beauty products and my Mum who I couldn't tell that I was expecting her first grandchild! (I wanted to tell her and my dad together as big reveal at Christmas).

The most nerve-wracking thing about a competition is the

other people! Being compared, awkward glances to see what each other are doing. Kicking yourself for not doing that cool thing that the therapist to the left of you is doing, just making silly mistakes. I remember my trousers being a bit too long and I hadn't taken them up and stupidly worrying that, that could be my down fall?! (Perfectionist Anxiety)

After a trades test and an interview with the judges. It was out of my hands. I could do no more other than use every LOA strategy I knew!

Here are some of the LOA strategies I tried. Give them a try when you are reaching for a particular goal:

- Create a vision board with desire, dream and goal. You want to create something that makes you feel excited when you look at it.
- Writing your main goal out every night before bed.
- Visualise your goal coming into fruition – How will you feel, who will you tell, how will it impact your life and those closest to you...imagine every tiny detail. For some reason as adults we forget the simple skill of pretend and daydream.
- Print your goal out and put it EVERYWHERE! Inside of draws, cars, wallets, screensavers.
- Change your passwords to include some clue of your goal, so it can trigger excitement.
- Meditate on it. Work on removing your self-doubt and any blocks.

- Listen to how you speak. Talk with certainty that you already have the particular thing.
- Have faith and know it is on its way.
- Work with oracle cards, talk to your Guides, Angels, The Universe, God, Spirit.
- Programme your crystals to help guide you and put them in your bra, purse, under your pillow. Anywhere they can fit, put one!
- Give gratitude. Write a gratitude list daily do as many as you feel drawn to do and even if you can only think of one thing put it down.

However, woo woo you want to go. I would say throw everything at it, what do you have to lose? The most important thing about working in this way is creating the FEELING and doing what you feel aligned to and what feels right.

It may take a couple of goes to find your thing. What you do not want to do, is do any of these things and just go through the motions and not feel connected to it. If what you are doing becomes a drag or a chore, then stop. It isn't a fail! Find your own way of feeling the magic and the flutter of excitement of what is coming. Trust your own instincts!

I went woo woo epically and it worked because in November 2016 after a fancy awards dinner in London, I was announced Beauty Therapist of The Year in front of 800 people from spas and salons around the world.

The feeling I got when I had invested so much energy, not

just practically but emotionally and mentally and it pays off, is literally something if I could bottle, I would be billionaire! It is blow your socks off, heart beating through your chest spectacular.

There were so many hurdles that I could have turned around and said "nope, not for me thanks. Not this year." I could have let my mind monkeys stop me. From people trying to discourage me to having to do an acceptance speech in front of 100's. But what a feeling I would have been doing myself out of! The thing that kept me going was the bigger picture. My WHY.

When you find your why, you will find your how

LIFE LESSON #3

Learn to follow your heart. Do not be swayed by others or even your subconscious. These are purely views to protect you and keep you comfortable. But in order to reach new levels and bathe in the glory of stepping closer and closer to where you want to be, getting comfortable with being uncomfortable is the only way.

Dealing with trauma

Healing come in waves and maybe today the wave hits rocks.

And that is OK, that's OK darling.

You are still healing

You are still healing

- Ijeoma Umebinyu

After I had won the award, work life was really good for a few years; I wrote for trade magazines, launched an online programme, collaborated with some great people in the industry, became a judge myself, got asked to talk on stage, was interviewed for podcasts and even was asked to go on live TV on The BBC's The One Show and mime my career to comedian Jack Whitehall so he could guess what I had won my award for. I shared the stage with the best; Toilet Cleaner of The Year, Grave Digger of The Year and Gas Fitter of The Year!! I know, I know - don't be too jealous!

Obviously during this time, I was pregnant, so I was made to slow down a bit from the physical part of the job. It was whilst I was pregnant, I started a blog. As a typical entrepreneur I love to create new stuff, so I was now ready to start thinking about the next BIG goal...to make money blogging and creating a You Tube channel. Using my skills as a therapist and a Pilates Instructor I wanted to bring self-care to Mum's to be and New Mum's. I invested and went on a women's business retreat and brainstormed my new business baby.

I created the brand, invested in an online blogging course and got going. The less I could work in my therapy room as I got bigger, the more time I invested in my blog. Not my You Tube channel as I was procrastinated on that, with too many self-inflicting reservations and wanting it to be perfect.

You know, I now strongly believe it is a perception that being a perfectionist is a strong character trait – who hasn't said in an interview when asked what is one of your strongest attributes? "A perfectionist, I love paying attention to very tiny detail". I know I have proudly too! Now being a business owner and now a coach I can now see it more of a hindrance. It can one of our biggest procrastination excuses and with no boss to okay what you have done or for you to be accountable too....great ideas just do not get shown to the world!

Waiting for the perfect moment may mean it never comes. I still have o subscribers to my You Tube channel! (It's something I'm working on!).

Anyway, I digress! I had a good pregnancy, actually pretty text book. I loved it for the most part and we both assumed once you have a baby life can just resume, a bit different yes. But you were still the same person, with the same goals, you just had a mini human to join the journey.

What no-one told me was actually having a baby, which I was extremely blessed with, would probably turn into the most challenging event of my life. Which with that brings a guilt that cuts so deep.

I would experience trauma like no pamper advert ever warned me about.

Don't get me wrong, I knew it wasn't going to pain free, but

I wanted it to be as calm as it could possibly be. We thrive on a no drama, calm life. We had sessions with a Hypno-birthing coach which was actually a life saver.

Shit hit the fan on labour day, which lasted for 70+ hours with a back to back baby, pressing on a nerve throughout every contraction (or "surge" as hypnotherapy calls them) in a July heatwave with the voice of a hypnotherapy woman; saying my cervix opened easily on REPEAT the entire time! (I have since deleted said audio for our sanity).

I now know my mind is bloody strong and the S.A.S had nothing on me on that day(s) and the power of the mind is absolutely incredible if called upon, it can get you through THE most gruelling of events. Ironically it wasn't the 70 hours that was the culprit for my trauma. It was probably the last 45-60 minutes and after Maddox was born, which caused me my trauma both mentally and physically.

That last hour was simply terrifying, I was out of control of my own body. I had had an emergency spinal tap, so although the pain had finally gone my legs were dead, it was like I was just watching what was happening to someone else, almost like an outer body experience. I was the most vulnerable I had ever been in my life and I had no way of stopping it.

The quietness of the operating room, the failed attempts to get him out, the anxious wait to hear your baby cry, the doctor saying, "I can't stop the blood". I truly felt like I was going to die, I just felt life was just slipping away in this cold, hardened, clinical place with people around me I didn't know. That was the start of my numbness.....when they placed Maddox on me I didn't feel the rush, the love they tell you about. I was exhausted and numb in every sense of the word.

I want to add here, I was told a few weeks later I was at no risk of dying. I think I was delirious from no sleep, losing about a litre of blood, no food, heat and pushing a baby out into the world!

After that life changing hour, a lot happened. We were in hospital for a week as I had to have the damage assessed from the array of implements used and just length of my labour. I had tests galore with fingers and probes put pretty much everywhere, panic attacks that paralysed me from moving, tremendous melt downs where I actually hid under the cover to escape. The hospital were great, but I felt completely violated by what had gone on. I was not prepared at all for any of what had happened and how I felt.

That hospital became my safe place, I made friends with the nurses, we had pretty much mini boot camp training of how to look after a baby, we had established a routine, we watched endless episodes of Practical Jokers and I didn't want to leave. I had almost become institutionalised in such a short time frame. My way of coping was humour through the numbness that would drift into the day in waves, some-times ones that just lap the shores gently to massive 30 ft ones that crashed down and consumed me.

I left to go home with a baby, injections to take daily, a

prolapsed womb, which felt like it was down to my knees and a catheter strapped to my leg for another 3 days AKA My Prada Piss Bag due to bladder and nerve damage. Ever tried to fashion one of those things? Yeah, you can't. With it comes anxieties, such as if the wind blows people will see my wee or if it over flows people will be covered in my wee! Neither are great options; both are cause for wonderful panic attacks! However, standing up to take a wee is life changing, so convenient!

As I read this back, I notice how I speak about being a first time Mum - unconnected. I was so consumed in my own thoughts, panic attacks, flash backs, anxiety, self-doubt, the lowest self-confidence I had ever known. I lost who I was, but I didn't have room in my head to be a Mum and look at what I had, I simply did not know how to.

I felt I had become a shadow of myself and felt like I couldn't connect properly with Maddox. I feel sad that I was not as present as I felt I should have been. Some days I would have to check in with myself to see how depressed I actually was by asking if I wanted to end my life - "Do I want to jump out of that window?". Thankfully it was always a no, but I knew that if I had a slight falter, I needed support quickly. There were a lot of days too that would be happy, and I felt confident with my ability of being the best mum. It wasn't all doom and gloom.

I didn't ever, not love Maddox that was never the issue. It was the trauma of what had happened to get him here and the days that followed. The feeling of love came slowly and got stronger every day. Now I love him, so much I cry when he eats peas as he is just such a beautiful soul. My every fibre aches with love for him. In the privacy of our own home we watch films of him on the TV, even when he is in the same room!

As the numbness passed and the horrific flashbacks stopped thanks to counselling, my emotions turned to anger and resentment. I mourned my old life like crazy. I felt more guilt for feeling like that. It was only when I was talking to a dear friend, she mentioned that I was going through the stages of mourning, and it clicked; I was literally going through them one by one.

The below are the stages designed by <u>Dr Elizabeth Dr. Kübler-Ross</u>

1. *Denial* – the numbness I felt the day I had Maddox was an epic WTAF!

2. *Anger* – I am not naturally an angry person, I find it an exhausting emotion, but I broke a lot of soft close mechanisms on our kitchen cupboards, cheddar cheese got lobbed down the hallway when I was alone many a time. I had so much resentment for my husband whose life seemed to go back to normal pretty much, but mine had changed to be unrecognisable.

3. *Bargaining* – I went back to my blog to try and help others going through similar. Sometimes it helped close doors, others I feel it stopped them from closing completely

and hindered the healing process and just kept opening up wounds. It allowed me closure.

4. *Depression* – Even a year plus later, I still had depressive thoughts, but it was more of a situational depression rather than clinical. After a friend told me some of my thoughts, such as being a parent is a life sentence were not "normal" I went to the Dr who put my mind at rest and told me that I was not clinically depressed.

They were just thoughts. My father has suffered clinical depression and anxiety for my whole life, I have grown up around it and seen what it can do to a person. I still 2 and a half years later still think being a parent is a life sentence! Of course, it is I will be his go-to person until my last breath, that is some responsibility! What I say or what I do now can impact his initial views of the world and himself for years! That's scary shit!

5. *Acceptance* – Eventually after the winter comes the spring. After the bleakest of winters, the hope of new beginnings and getting my head around this new life situation started to happen. Finding new ways to deal with circumstances, the heaviness lifted, and joy started to fill up my life bit by bit.

As I was writing this part, I took lots of procrastination breaks and pulled an oracle card from Rebecca Campbell Work Your Light Oracle Cards to help give me guidance...

I pulled the Transformation card – Things are changing at a cellular level. Deep Healing. (I know, how uncanny!).

"Things are changing at a cellular level. You are not who you were a year ago or who you will soon be. You are in between, emerging, half risen, half falling. Keep doing the work, you are transforming.

You will look back at this time with awe. So much is happening in your inner world and within your cells. It's time to release old ways of being that have kept you in fight-flight-freeze mode. Choose a new way of being, where trauma is not the driving force....."

Grief can hit us about anything we lose, not just a loved one, but a job, a relationship, a way of living. I felt so lost. I lost my freedom and my control of my day. I was lonely, full of self-scrutiny, had lack of self-worth in abundance. I had gone from someone doing what they loved, loved what they were creating, following a calling that had been pulling me for years...to being skint, in pain, anxious about what others thought, totally winging how to bring up a baby, stressed about doing the right thing, bored and thrown into groups of people that I had nothing in common with about apart from a baby.

It seems to be a thing around new Mums that no-one speaks the truth. I have always been honest. I never hid how I felt, even when that made some uncomfortable. One lady at a sing and song class I went to asked how I was getting on; I replied with the only honest answer I had "okay, but I really struggled at first. I didn't really like it much to start with" her reply. "God, your honest!". After that I didn't really go to many groups, they were just full of people saying how much they love it and talking about how much their baby weighed and looking at me like I was the bad one for not taking him to be weighed enough. My philosophy he pooed, he ate, he slept, he was happy, he was growing out of his clothes - Job done!

It was like he knew Mum was struggling and he was so laid back and when I look back he was a complete joy. I wish I could remember some of those days and feel so selfish that I was lost in how I felt. But my husband says he can't remember much either (but is that just men?) and assured me that I wasn't a walking "F**K My Life Zombie", which is a win in my eyes. That makes me feel lighter to know that Maddox would not have known the demons going on in my thoughts, for that I am grateful.

So here we are 2.5 years in, and I have accepted and love my new life. My fear of going through it again is too strong to ever have more children. I am an only child myself. I am at peace with having no more. We have a great little family and I love pretty much every minute of it now. The other night my husband said imagine if it was all a dream and we hadn't had him, in a heartbeat I would go through it all again. I just couldn't not have my little ray of sunshine in my life. It was worth the journey. As cliché as it sounds time is a healer.

LIFE LESSON #4

Being kind to yourself.

Know life comes in seasons. From a bleak winter, a hopeful spring is on its way.

I now have a go-to kit of strategies in place to recognise when old feelings return, when funkiness is creepy in, when overwhelm starts to drown me. The next winter season will come, it may be in a year it maybe 10. But that is life, the highs, the lows, the twists and turns. I understand now that these winters are sent to teach us. We grow stronger, we become more resilient, they make us step into our power, to rise up when we have fallen.

Be mindful with yourself and ask in these challenging times "okay, what is the lesson here? What I am to learn from this?"

Recognising the signs that you are heading into a vulnerable space, can help you to deal with the issues sooner, this could just make your winter period a lot shorter than it needs to be. Sometimes you cannot do it alone and it is okay to ask for help. It is not a sign of weakness.

I find journaling to be a helpful tool at times of anxiety, stress and overwhelm.

Here are some prompts that you can try, if you do not know where to start..

1. How am I feeling right now?

2. What surprises me about my life right now?

3. What would I do if I knew I could not fail?

4. How do I feel regards my finances, my friendships, my relationships, my work, my body, my mind?

5. What isn't serving my right now?

6. What am I afraid of? What is the worst outcome?

7. What is going right?

8. What am I grateful for?

9. What do I want to achieve?

10. Who do I need to be, in order to do the things I want to do? How can I start to be that person right now?

11. What do I love about myself?

12. What's the kindest things you can do for yourself when you are in a place of pain, anxiety, depression, overwhelm, stress?

13. How can I love myself better today?

Either you run the day, or the day runs you – Jim Rohn

Starting your day, the right way sets you up to either to win the day or regret the day. I used to hate mornings. The alarm would go on snooze for probably 30 minutes, then some procrastination time on social media, looking at what Shelia from Dallas did when she went out last weekend. Bubble-gum for the brain. Then a mad rush to get ready and no-doubt just turning up in the nick of time. Then add a baby into the mix the morning can either drag with loneliness, kids' TV durge in the background or it goes so fast you haven't even brushed your teeth, let alone win the morning as well!

It is exhausting living life in a rush, wasting precious moments on activities that do not enrich your day. Sometimes we do need bubble-gum TV and just to schedule in NOTHING time. It is important, I'm all for taking time out. However, when it starts to become a procrastination activity that gets longer and longer and stops you doing the things that can drive you forward into the direction of your dreams then something needs to change.

LIFE LESSON #5

Get up, feed your brain & soothe your soul

It is all about the morning routine, and once you establish one that you feel aligned to, you may just start loving mornings and feel excited about getting up! I actually do now, so if I can, so can you!

Now for me, these early starts (and to some this may not be early at all!) took some getting used and I had to ease myself into it. My alarm was Maddox, but I now love getting up before everyone else and just doing things for me. I use an app to block my phone from 9.30pm to 8.30am so I cannot use any social media or receive messages and I get the breakfast stuff ready and load the washing machine the night before. This time of day is my time to gather my thoughts, get prepared for the day and focus on my goals.

A typical morning of mine

- Wake up 6/6.30am. I now wake up naturally at this time, so do not set an alarm. If I sleep, then I honour that my body needs it.
- Drink hot lemon and water (made the night before, put in a flask and taken up to bed).
- Listen to You Tube guided meditation for 10-20 minutes – depending on my mood and what's going on. It could be an abundance meditation, gratitude, chakra balancing, connecting with my angels, positivity etc.
- I have an affirmation that I speak out whilst doing a power pose (the idea being you move around to the energy flowing) and inhaling an essential oil such as Frankincense, Neroli, Ylang Ylang.
- Look at my Pinterest Vision Board or my vision board on the wall for 10 minutes and visualise these things coming into fruition.
- Listen to an audio book or do some kind of self-development work such as learn about crystals, do some crafting etc.
- Get up and get ready for the day.

Just say yes, you never know where it may take you

I have had many attempts over the years to start beauty businesses way before social media was what it is now. I had all the gear and no idea. Literally. I dabbled in various ideas with no pricing structure, no marketing or no brand. I made a lot of mistakes and had my confidence knocked many a time on this entrepreneurial journey. The one thing I want to leave with you in my chapter is to feel the fear and do it anyway.

Yes, you will make mistakes. Yes, you may have to make sacrifices. Yes, some will be a waste of time and even a waste of money. But you fail forwards. It is all progress. Take risks, do things that scare you and enjoy this mad journey.

Being crystal clear on your WHY, will help push you when times are tough, and procrastination is the easy answer. If you focus on your WHY every day, it will make you push your own boundaries. You will push limits you didn't think you could, as you have that finish line in sight.

LIFE LESSON #6

Fear stops more dreams that failure ever will.

STOP putting excuses in the way, to stop you moving forwards. Do not be ashamed of who you are, what you stand for, what you have created, what you look like or how you sound. It all tends to be down to that 4 letter word FEAR....

Fear of what others will think.

Fear that you are not good enough.

Fear that you do not know enough.

Fear that you are not like Sandra up the road.

Fear you will fail.

START saying yes.

Start saying yes to new opportunities.

Start saying yes to that great idea you had the other night, rather than talking yourself out of it with all the "what ifs".

Start making connections with people that you know will help push your idea forward.

When you have an idea and those little mind monkeys start rearing up their ugly head and start talking you out of it. Silence them and ask yourself "What is the worst that can really happen?" If the worst that can happen doesn't fill with you with complete dread and you can deal with the outcome...then maybe you should just go for it!

If nothing else, you gave it a go. You tried it; you add to the "I experienced it" list. Who cares if it didn't work out or you didn't like it as much as you thought? At least you tried. I would rather try and fail than stay where I am; unhappy and day dreaming about a future I desire.

You are capable of greatness. It is now time for you to start seeing and believing that for yourself. I believe in you and I am excited for what is to come!

ABOUT THE AUTHOR

KERRY BEAVIS

Kerry Beavis is an award winning Beauty Therapist, a mentor to solotherapists; empowering them to have successful therapy businesses via The Revive Co. Pro, a course creator and trainer at her beauty school - The Revive Co. Beauty Academy, a self-care junkie, a crystal collector, posh food eater and Mum to 2.5 years old Maddox and Wife to the man-child Rob.

After setting up an at home beauty & holistic treatment room and running Pilates classes in 2012, she later became Beauty Therapist of The Year 2016.

She loves to say yes to new opportunities and experiences. This has helped her be on national TV, the front cover of a magazine, write for top trade magazines, judge for industry awards, speak at events, meet some fabulous people, learn new skills and see the world (although there is a lot more to see!) and have stories to tell her grandkids.

Kerry now spends her time being a Mum, treating a small loyal client base; specialising in massage, Pilates and Facials and coaching therapists to be amazing and fulfil their dreams and desires through 1-2-1 programmes and online courses.

"My aim is help therapists become more successful than me. Nothing beats helping a coaching client or a student reach new goals, that they thought they could never reach. People inspire me every day and I am humbled to be a small part of their journey to living their dream experience"

Kerry has been a beauty therapist for 15 years. After quitting university, studying jewellery design, she realised although she loved being creative, she didn't have the passion nor the drive to take her into a successful career, so she changed paths at 21.

She has always pushed herself to learn more, experience more and to be amongst the best. Having invested in all sorts of training from therapies, teacher training, Pilates Instructor training, how to write a blog, funnels, sales, how to create an online course, marketing.

She loves to learn and loves to teach. She was teaching

"how to.." Make Up fun days even whilst she was still studying at college!

Her moto is to feel the fear and do it anyway. Amazing things can happen if you just say yes!

Find Kerry on social media, she would love to connect with you!

Facebook Personal Page – Kerry Beavis

Facebook Group – Therevivecopro

Instagram – kb_the_beauty_expert

Linkedin - kerry-beavis-b495776a

www.therevivecopro.com

7 Lessons to Stepping into your Greatness

"Turn your wounds into wisdom."

— **Oprah Winfrey**

I couldn't have said that any better, life is one hell of a roller-coaster in fact at times life can be seen as one huge volcano about to erupt, but every experience I truly believe is put in front of us for a reason and that is for a lesson to be learned.

You are about to read some snippets from my life and how I have turned those events in my life towards good and light. If there is one gift I would like you to take from reading this, it is how you can flip your mind and your thoughts in the direction of pushing you for the change in your life you want NOW.

Lesson 1 – YOUR THOUGHTS CREATE YOUR REALITY.

I have used my life experiences to date to build not just my businesses but my life. I am the, Mother, Wife, Daughter, Sister, Auntie and Business Woman because of these experiences.

I have used wherever possible every event, circumstance and hurdle that I have had to jump as a sign of "this is happening for a reason" not "why is this happening to me?" don't get me wrong I have certainly said the latter, who hasn't? but over time I have been quicker each time to snap out of victim mode and try and figure out what I have to do to get me to where I ideally want to be.

If I can give you any comfort right now before you carry on reading I would like to say this. Where ever you are in your life right now, whatever is happening, if you are struggling in any way, I am here to say now, stick in there because I truly believe what that struggle is today, will certainly be your strength tomorrow and you will be ok. However awful it maybe at the time, and I know it can be so painful at times, you can survive, and YOU WILL if you stay focused on the outcome you want.

That is the power of your thoughts, taking the steps to

ensure that you do get the reality you wish for. I am not going to say it is easy, I have had to work on the skill of determination, tenacity and resilience every day and it's an ongoing process for me. Every new level I reach there is something I have to figure out. "Another level, Another Devil" I don't think hurdles and events just stop like that in your life because you have reached that next level of financial independence or the next life achievement.

Every step we take up that staircase there is something we have to get over to reach the next step it's just how you react to each and every step you take. Every time I make more money, or I commit to something new there is another fear, or challenge that slips in I need to deal with. This is when power of positivity is key to ensure you are always building.

I can tick many things off a list titled "ADVERSITY" and so many of us can fall into the trap of feeling stuck, or ill-educated on not knowing the "how" to move forward or worse continue to play the victim and just stay put, sometimes complaining and dwelling what is going on at the time.

Those that do this may not realise they are doing it, but it doesn't do anyone any favours in doing so. Making excuses or feeling you can never be the person you want to be are just thoughts and feelings you can change. This is something I have understood simply as pesky beliefs.

Have you ever seen someone talented just... not quite make it? It seems like things haven't worked in their favour...Well I'm willing to put money on this explanation: they weren't set up with the mindset to take them to the levels they should have reached. We all have to face obstacles that aren't in our favour. And we have to get through them and past them. If you surrender to your unfortunate circumstances that's where your growth will stop right there.

Summary

• Focus on what you want NOT what you don't want. This will breed positivity and it will get stronger over time as the results you want become a reality.

• Thoughts and feelings are just that, "pesky beliefs" find the strength and process to reverse them into steps towards the outcome you want.

• Whatever your struggle is today I promise you it will be your strength tomorrow and finding solutions will get easier, but you have to make the effort to find them.

Lesson 2 – ALWAYS FOLLOW YOUR INTUITION

I feel we are always being put in front of cross roads, constantly being asked the question, "are you going to deal with it in this way and start this path?" or "are you going to go this way?" All I wanted was a good life, to not have to worry about money, to love others to be loved, and to love myself. You see, I have always felt different in some way, like I am an old soul, thinking to ahead for my years at times.

But also, having a gut instinct that I know what people are thinking, intuitive is the word I suppose. I can look at a photo or see someone sending me a text and I have this intuition or have this "knowing" they are not quite telling me the truth. Or they are smiling but they are not at all feeling that smile they have.

This has proven to be a great skill over the last 11 years as an Entrepreneur, I can sit across a table from people and have this gut feeling they are bending the truth and I can turn the conversation around that enables me not to make a commitment that could later burn me. At the same time, I have a good inkling when I think someone means well when others think not, and I love it when those I had faith in prove me right. This all started when I was young and following that intuition more over the years has now helped me have a relationship with my Father that I thought I would never have.

I am the eldest of three daughters and my parents divorced when I was young. We experienced many troubled times due to the marriage my mother and father had. I believe at some point before I was born they truly loved each other, well at least liked each other, my mother was training as a nurse and my father was a policeman, but I don't recall ever seeing them love each other. I always sensed hurt, anger and jealousy, and I never understood why, in fact to this day I still don't understand what happened.

My first memory believe it or not, was when I was just over two years old and my father was in an armchair asleep whilst my middle sister was being born in hospital. I remember trying to walk up the stairs, I was on the bottom step at the time and I was thinking how my dad was asleep and I need to get up these stairs, (I know it's hard to believe but as I write this now, I feel I am back in that moment).

My nappy was so wet, and I recall feeling really uncomfortable. It's amazing I remember snippets of my life when I was so young, but I believe there is a very good reason for this. This memory is actually a nice one as my gut tells me every time I think back at this time this is a moment with me and my dad whatever reality was going on at the time it was him and me.

I had my father in my life until I was 11 and then not again until I was 24 then lost contact again when I was 26. I eventually took the step to contact him again when I was 36 because my gut is always telling me, he is not the perfect Dad, but he does love you in his way. In life or in business I listen to that repeated voice that pops in my head and it always helps me grow both in business and in life. My dad to this day has never met his grandchildren but I know I am meant to have him in my life in some way. Following your intuition in my experience has got me to re build so many parts of my life, with money and with relationships.

My father as I say is not perfect, he never sends me a birthday card, the last time I saw him I was 26, but my intuition tells me every day that he is meant to be in my life and whatever wrongs he has done I know he loves me and my middle sister and no relationship has to be perfect. That early memory is one compared to others you will read that has helped me remember to follow my gut and not always listen to others and their experiences. Listen to yourself and what your heart and gut is telling you sometimes it will get you a lot further than not.

Summary

• You have intuition for a reason, you need to trust it and not depend always on others.

• Other people experiences are not yours.

• Get your Intel and then decide what the best result is for you. Who will it serve, and does it help your journey?

Lesson 3 - EMBRACE FEAR TO A POINT THAT IT FUELS YOU TO TAKE MASSIVE ACTION

My father, for his reasons alone will know why, he drank and as a result my mother was scared most of the time. We were always told "don't tell your daddy this, don't tell your daddy that". I am not here to say my father is the bad person or my mother but whatever the circumstances, it was not a healthy marriage and there were so many moments that myself and my middle sister felt alone and scared and fear like never before.

Let me ask you, have you ever wanted something so badly

that FEAR stops you OR have you ever been in a situation that you are scared of the outcome and wonder can I do anything about this?

One moment for me was when my mum and dad were arguing, I think I was about 5 or 6 and my middle sister was 3 or 4. I remember my Dad was very drunk and there was a lot of fear. We lived in a lovely village in Sabden, Lancashire, and it's a house I always think of from time to time for some reason. What I can say about this moment is that I was scared big time. My mum is holding my sister by the kitchen door and my dad is about to do something. The next moment I see my mum run out to the back yard with my sister. I am standing there behind my dad frozen. Someone had been hurt because I could see blood on my sister's nose.

I am feeling panic and real fear. Why has my mum run without me? I am worried and in hindsight I know my dad would not hurt me, but I didn't really know him. In fact, if I am truly honest I still don't, though I do try with our monthly telephone calls. There is this big tall man and I am wondering is he going to hurt me, and I need to move, but I can't move, I AM FROZEN.

My dad would never have hurt me, I know that now and in his own way I know he loves his daughters but at the time with everything going on, the screaming, people getting hurt I just wanted to run, and I wanted to get out of the house.

We all feel fear. It's nothing to shy away from. But you can't let it sit in the driver's seat. Fear is coming for the ride, but it's staying in the backseat whilst you steer your journey.

I have always taken this experience as an opportunity to get me to where I need to be both in life and business.

You see I felt so much energy inside me, the adrenalin, I embraced it and I ran past my dad, I ran outside as fast as I could and felt triumph that I'd got to my destination, to my mum and sister.

In business and in life when you are fearful of that next step when you are so scared and worried about what could go wrong, what will be the outcome? I remember this early memory of fear, because it reminds me that I can always stand still and do nothing, or do I move and go for it?

Summary

• You can use your experiences how to relegate FEAR to the backseat and use these memories or visions as the fuel to move you forwards.

• You are in control of your mindset so you CAN regulate that FEAR. You've got to learn how to adjust it so that your mind is working WITH you and not against you.

• Use Fear as a tool to get you moving not stopping you so you're standing still.

Lesson 4 - ADAPTABILITY AND RESILIENCE TO CHANGE, WILL HELP YOU GROW

Looking back, although I love my mother and father I don't feel they ever put their daughters first. It was always their hatred and their indulgences that came first. My mother loves her children, but she has, and I feel still does crave a certain lifestyle today which halts the true relationship I would like with my mother. I feel very responsible for her and I worry about her.

Of course, what daughter doesn't, and I believe she is my mother for a reason - to learn and ensure that I don't take the same actions she has and to have the relationship with my own daughter I wish we'd had. I miss my mother every day and the simple things like calling to check you are ok, is something I still crave in my late 30's but the lesson is you can only have responsibility for your own actions not others' and coming from a place of love is far better than bitterness. There is something we can always take and make good and light in our lives moving forward - though at times it can still hurt.

At aged seven my sister and I ended up in foster care separated from our mother and forced to stay with people we really did not want to be with. Again, we had to change schools, meet new people and leave more friends behind. Our father did not take us in for reasons only he knows about, and there were no other family members who could take us. I remember it was School Sports day and the teacher called for both my middle sister and I to come to the bottom of the field. I had this feeling something was not right because that very morning when we said goodbye to mum she was sat very smartly dressed and not looking happy at all. I felt so much worry and sadness.

She could hardly say "good bye" to us both and just sat there legs crossed, and I remember giving her a kiss on the lips with my eyes open as were hers thinking "I am not going to see you later". That thought passed throughout the day until the moment came when the teacher called for us. I remember clear as day as if I am there right now, feeling nervous, saying to my sister we are going to be ok. When we were in the Headmasters office he sat calmly and explained that mum was going away for some time and they were not sure when we will see her again, but they were trying to find someone to look after us.

This was the first time I did not cry. I held it all in. I remember putting my left arm around my sister and saying, "its ok I will look after you, I won't let anything happen to you", at the same time trying my hardest not to cry. Bravery is tough, so is responsibility and this was the moment I took the word responsibility to another level. We had to adapt very quickly, meet new friends, attend another school and wait for the moment we were picked up to visit our mother.

All in all, it was 6 months when we were reunited again with mum. We lived in a rough area where we had cockroaches in the kitchen of the house we were staying in. To be honest I didn't mind as we were all back together again. But happiness was not forever. I was stealing and lying, and I was lost. I didn't know what to do or how to feel. My sister and I always fought and one day it was too much for mum.

She said, "Maybe you should go and live with your Dad". So, at aged 10, I stayed with my father and my step-mum and frankly made the biggest mistake I could leaving my mother and sister.

I thought the grass was greener but in true honesty it really was not. The only people who were nice to me were my eldest step-sister, Dad and my Nana who I loved very much. Actually that was the best part, my Nana lived down the hill and I loved seeing her. She was my closest grandparent and to this day (although she has passed many years ago) there is not a day I don't think about her. Unfortunately, I was not wanted at my Dad's I feel now my Dad was torn trying to do the right thing, but his wife was not keen and I was not easy.

My other step-sister bullied me and actually had me beaten up by the next-door neighbour. I remember at the time my step-sister was standing on our doorstep laughing with her friend as I was getting kicked in the tummy and I never told a soul. That I can tell you now is why I am so anti-bullying and have zero tolerance for it as of course most do. My step-mum just gave me dirty looks every opportunity she could. I give her compassion and I really do respect any woman or man that takes on another person's child, I can imagine it can be difficult, but dirty looks and feeling unwanted really did not help me.

At the same time I found out that my mother was pregnant with my little sister and had to go away once again. This time my middle sister was in foster care and I had no way to go back to them. I felt lost and my father would not let me visit my mum and my sister refused to come to our Dad. At this point I was extremely unhappy.

I had to adapt every day and make this work, to try and see the end result and that was when I would be able to see my mum again. The time eventually arrived, and I had to make a decision and I had to choose between my mother and father.

My mother told me that if I wanted to live with her and my two sisters then I would need to run away, and I would never see them again including my Nana. I will never forget that last time I saw my Nana and had to say goodbye. She always stood at her side gate to wave to me whilst I walked up the hill but this time I stopped, and I looked back and I remember saying to myself "I am so sorry Nana". Only a few months earlier she had lost my Uncle John to a car accident.

He was only 38 and now she was losing her only grandchildren. This was another moment in my life when I would make sure history would never repeat. At the age of 11, I felt that these two humans that had myself and my sister were still putting their hatred before us, and frankly we had both had enough.

I went to many primary schools and moved house many times. As a result of this, as an adult I never find moving house stressful because I have done it so many times as a child. In addition to this meeting new people is something I find very easy to do. I believe what has got me

REBECCA CROSS | 291

through some of these events is adaptability and resilience.

In business you need to adapt and be resilient, market changes, your ideal client may change but you need to ensure whatever is thrown at you, you can adapt and work with. The events above were tough, and I had to adapt every day to ensure I got through to the next. I have taken this skill and growth to the next level of helping me work with many other women and build businesses.

Thinking out of the box, not making excuses just good old-fashioned action. Sometimes life does not work out, but that should never stop you going for what you want - EVER! What many find difficult is that not everything will stay the same and you can never be complacent. If you can accept, adapt, and find a way to make this better for you, in life and in business, you will fly!

Summary

• To build and to move forward we have to go with the changes and those that do will go further than those that do not.

• Practice moving out of your comfort zone daily as complacency is not the ideal place to be working from at any time.

Lesson 5 - GRATITUDE

I struggled in education. I was bottom in most classes and

was always thinking, "how the heck am I going to survive?" I still, to this day have no Maths qualification and I still do not know my times table. There are many words in my basic vocabulary I don't understand, and I am known for saying lots of words backwards, but it is something I have learned to work on and in the past have tried to hide. I don't think jumping from one school to another helped, I remember thinking my brain simply works a different way.

My middle sister went to the same number of schools as me and she is so clever, she could put her mind to anything but me I just didn't get things. I am a very visual person though and the one skill I used to love with a passion at school was Art and that is something I knew I could do easily.

My step-father was in the army and an opportunity arose for my middle sister and I to go to boarding school. I was not there long - less than 3 years as my mum and step-father could not pay the fees, and so just before my GCSE's exams were about to start we were asked to leave.

This was the one time that in all the schools I have attended and left, leaving this one in particular was not just hard but embarrassing. The school agreed to allow me to return to sit my exams, but I was not allowed to sit the exams wearing my school uniform as I was no longer a pupil there. This was a moment I remembered gratitude, a moment I remembered to be thankful for the opportunity. I wrote a letter to the Head Master to thank him for his school and the experiences I had and that I was grateful that I had been allowed to return for my exams, as this I imagine was at the school's cost, not my parents.

Gratitude is something I have practised more and more over the last 11 years but looking back there were many moments I practised it as a child without realising and believe me this helped me get through so many situations. Another was when we lived in the South of the UK and my school was in the North of the UK, so I came home for a short amount of time.

My mum put me on a train on my own to travel 6 hours to stay with a teacher who kindly let me stay to revise whilst I set the exams. I remember having to be so brave. I needed to do these exams so I would get into the local college to do the next level of education. All my friends were from a more abundant life than myself, and to be honest were not very kind. No one would speak to me and I was the only one in my own clothes and everyone knew why.

This was a moment in my life where I thought I will never get through this. I am thick, I have struggled, and I do not know where I am heading. I am nearly 16 years old and I can never see me ever being successful or rich. Then I had to do what I have done many times - feel that fear and think about being brave but to be thankful for the situation. You see I feel bravery is when you believe enough in the unbelievable. When others judge you or place their doubt on you.

You say I KNOW I can do this; I KNOW I will succeed. I had no idea how those exams were going to pan out, but I got this far on my own and the Head-master of the school had given me an opportunity when he didn't have to. You see I feel most people try to achieve the goals they feel are safe and "big enough" but not massive or even inconceivable! These exams were the latter. It was not just the exams it was the goal of being there in that environment for the days I was there. Dealing with the shame I felt back then, not now. This was where my tenacity started to kick in, my determination and to be kind to others and treat them with compassion.

Gratitude is the number one lesson I practise daily - if I have a client or if I gain a saving somewhere, or if I park in a carpark and someone gives me their car park ticket with money still left on, anything at all I am grateful. During the past 11 years building businesses this one lesson has got me very far and I know it's something that has helped me from a very young age.

Summary

• Gratitude can be for those times that are good and bad. It's a moment to be grateful that something is ending, and something is starting.

• It may be time for change, or this loss is to be a lesson.

• Always thank even the small things that happen you never know what big things will grow.

. . .

Lesson 6 – YOU WANT THAT DREAM THEN GO AND GET IT!

When I was 14 at boarding school they realised I had a learning difficulty, and it was confirmed I was dyslexic with a reading age of seven. That was the start of the Rebecca you would meet today.

Fast forward a few years, I ended up working so hard on my education, hard enough to pursue a university degree. I realised that with the right people around me and the right mindset you truly can achieve ANYTHING. I had other events start creeping in again that were equally painful as a child. I lost my middle sister for some time to addiction and I was trying to help her the best I could, but she simply does not want the help. I have not seen her since my daughter was born in 2008 and would love to see her again as I do miss her. Like many lessons in life I have learned the skill of patience and I understand when the time is right for events the time is right, and I believe every day we will see each other again, and I visualise the huge smile on our faces and love we still have for each other.

I was 15 when I met my first love. He and his family truly took me under their wing. I was able to experience what being with a "normal" family was like. We married 10 years later. However, what I didn't realise is that the Rebecca who had grown up with feelings of survival and that kick-ass attitude had become lost somewhere in comfort and being looked after and had forgotten so much of how she got to where she was heading.

Despite my unsettling childhood, I left university worked for amazing corporates like IBM and the Wall Street Journal. But my kick-ass attitude had now vanished. I was comfortable and not living the true life I know I was destined for. When I was 27 years old, I gave birth to my daughter Emily. And then, totally unexpected, two weeks later and not long after my 28th birthday, my husband walked out on Emily and I.

At this time I did not even know how to pay an electricity bill, never mind change a nappy. I was not the true me. I was lost, I was scared, and I hardly told anyone that I was on my own for 12 months. Family did not know for nearly 6 months I truly did not want history to repeat itself.

However, when Emily was about 4 weeks old that old Rebecca was surfacing slowly, I was crying every day but the Rebecca who found out at 14 she had a reading age of 7, the one that made sure she would make a life for herself and be a kick-ass no-nonsense woman was coming back! So that is what I did. I started my first kitchenware business. It was online and I spent a fortune on my Barclaycard to set the website up. I promised Emily I would be a millionaire and would be a mother she would be proud of and look up to. I was determined not to have history repeat itself.

This business went relatively well for a few years. I didn't make a lot of money at all, I mean really it was not anything to brag about, but the losses I made were certainly the lessons I learned. When Emily was nearly 12 months old, I started a magazine business. This went really well. I eventually sold it, and this gave me the opportunity to invest in another venture which was a franchise and I set up as Virtual Assistant.

This is funny because I am a rubbish VA and I was very much focused on my skillset with this business, and that was selling. If you want to run a business focus on what you are good at, outsource the rest. This business turned out really well when I was working part-time and generating 5.5k a month. It fitted perfectly around the babies. I had my son Finlay in 2013, 6 months after setting up the VA business and in May 2014 I had Henry around the same time my next venture my first property business was set up.

In 2016 my VA business transitioned over to my Mentoring and Coaching business I have today "Stepping into Greatness". These two companies are the businesses that I am growing today, and I truly love what I do.

I realised when I started studying Motivation and NLP and then Theta Healing, I have this skill to build businesses by using authentic strategies that fit that individual and frankly is not bull sh#t it works!

I have the great privilege to mentor a number of VAs in the Virtual Assistant market for a global online business (the franchise I invested in many years ago) working on their business strategy and supporting living the true work-life balance.

I want to be honest here: entrepreneurship is not an easy ride. In fact hell, not just entrepreneurship, life is not easy.

We all have a story and we all have events that have had an impact on our lives. But it really is how you view those events and how you react which will be the making of you.

I have realised that anything is truly possible. I have two companies that are on their way to generating nearly half of a million dollars moving into 2019. My journey to help 2 million women is truly on its way. I have remarried and he is a man that supports my journey and I am grateful for him every day; I have three beautiful children and I truly love me.

I have realised that my individuality is so important to me, to my family and friends and to those I serve. Why? Because we are all unique and we are all here for a reason. It stems from our passion, what we strive to do in life and what we truly desire. If you can tap into that and work on that you can achieve truly magnificent things, and this is so important.

Summary

• You want it stop the excuses and find a way.

• Only YOU can make it happen.

• This is YOUR life believe, trust and take action.

Lesson 7 – BE AUTHENTIC AND THE TRUE VERSION OF YOU!

There is another important lesson I want to share, and this

has helped me hugely, to make the money I make and build the relationships I have today.

When I was growing up I was called so many different things: "gob-a-lot" (because I talked too much), "I talked too loud", "I have a big bum", "I am not all there", "I have a potty mouth" I could go on but I have learned that these are not my faults - these are my gifts and I take these forward as the person I am today.

I urge you to take steps to be the true you - always. If you're not aligned with your authentic self, nothing is easy. You're wasting energy moderating and monitoring yourself and trying to be someone else. I remember as a child all the different schools, the different places we lived, that this is a new start I will try and not be the person I am being told I am.

I will be honest; it was exhausting. When I started offering myself to others exactly as I was, how I was made, how I have been defined by my own actions and thoughts, when I started to accept my background, my personality, qualities and differences, I realized all of these things I am, I am for a reason. You might not feel like you fit in, but no two pieces of a puzzle are to be the same for you to build that bigger picture.

Summary

• Be the best version of you that is the authentic you, the warts and all, being true to you and coming from love and light is one of the many important ingredients of success and you will attract what you put out every single time.

• Be grateful for every single event in your life.

I certainly am and for my parents for the people they were then and are now. I love them for that because I would certainly not be the Rebecca that I am today!

Wishing you so much luck and love!

ABOUT THE AUTHOR

REBECCA CROSS

Rebecca Cross is a kickass award-winning Business Success and Motivational Strategist and serial entrepreneur. She currently runs two businesses - a property business, and a mentoring and coaching business which are heading towards a combined turnover of half a million dollars.

Rebecca's positive mindset and attitude has enabled her to plough through life and beat the odds. She has huge determination, tenacity, and resilience that stems from her childhood of foster care, addiction, and overcoming a reading age of 7 when she was 14 years old.

As a Motivational Map Business Practitioner, NLP (neuro-linguistic programming) Practitioner, and Theta Healing Practitioner, Rebecca not only mentors and coaches nearly 100 VAs worldwide, but also motivates and inspires hundreds of women in her global Facebook community 'Stepping into Greatness'. Her message is that with accountability and support (if needed) they can achieve anything they put their mind to.

A mum-of-three and a keen runner, Rebecca's lifelong mission is to help two million women to step into their greatness. She totally believes in authentic and no bull sh#t business strategies and loves to build and work with budding entrepreneurs who are at the beginning of their business journey.

Contact:

Website: http://www.rebeccacrossltd.com

Facebook Group: https://www.facebook.com/groups/795266393986875/

Instagram: https://www.instagram.com/rebeccaanncross/

LinkedIn: https://www.linkedin.com/in/rebecca-cross-steppingintogreatness/